QUOTATIONS

for

SPEECHES

QUOTATIONS

for

SPEECHES

JOHN DAINTITH
ANNE STIBBS

BLOOMSBURY

This edition published 1992

Copyright © Bloomsbury Publishing Limited
Bloomsbury Publishing Limited, 2 Soho Square, London W1V 5DE

Extracts from the Authorized King James Version of the Bible, which is Crown Copyright, are reproduced by permission of Eyre and Spottiswoode, Her Majesty's Printers.

British Library Cataloguing in Publication Data

A CIP catalogue record for this book is available from the British Library

ISBN 0 7475 1433 X

Complied and typeset by
Market House Books, Ltd., Aylesbury
Printed in Great Britain by
Clay Ltd, St Ives PLC

CONTENTS

Acknowledgments

Editors

John Daintith
Anne Stibbs

Contributors

Fran Alexander
Elizabeth Bonham
Alan Isaacs
Jonathan Law
Sandra McQueen
Elizabeth Martin
Jessica Scholes
Gwen Shaw
Brenda Tomkins
Linda Wells
Edmund Wright

INTRODUCTION

This book is a collection of over 1000 quotations designed to be used by anyone who wants to make or write a speech. The quotations have been chosen for their aptness or wit or their relevance to a particular topic.

The first part of the book has a short section of quotations about speeches and speech making. Then follows the main body of the quotations, arranged under a series of topic headings. These headings appear in alphabetical order. A list of the topics is given overleaf. Under each topic heading, the quotations are numbered and arranged in alphabetical order by the author's name.

Two indexes appear at the end of the book to help the user. The first is based on the *keyword* or *-words* in a quotation. This index will be of use to anyone who can remember part of a quotation and wishes to locate it and check its source. The second index is a *name index*, useful for those seeking appropriate quotations by their favourite writers or speakers. Both indexes, direct the reader to the topic under which the quotation appears and to its number.

Of course, people who make or write speeches should use their own words; it is, however, sometimes useful to have help. As Anatole France said, 'When a thing has been said and said well, have no scruple. Take it and copy it.'

We hope that this book will be useful to people who have no scruples about saying things well.

The Editors

LIST OF TOPICS

Morality
Mortality
Music
Nakedness
Noncommitment
Obesity
Obituaries
Occupations
Opportunity
Optimism
Parties
Past
Patriotism
Peace
Perfection
Pessimism
Places
Pleasure
Popularity
Poverty
Power
Practicality
Praise
Prayer
Prejudice
Present
Principles
Progress

Promises
Promptness
Pronunciation
Prophecy
Public
Purity
Regret
Religion
Reputation
Responsibility
Ridicule
Right
Royalty
Ruthlessness
Sarcasm
Science
Self-control
Selflessness
Self-made men
Self-preservation
Seriousness
Sex
Simplicity
Sincerity
Sleep
Smoking
Snobbery

Sorrow
Speech
Sport
Success
Superstition
Support
Survival
Taxation
Technology
Temptation
Theatre
Thinking
Time
Trust
Truth
Uncertainty
Understanding
Universe
Verbosity
Vice
Virtue
Weapons
Weddings
Wisdom
Women
Work
Youth

SPEECHES

Some quotations about speaking in public

Introductions

Ways to start a speech?

1 If there are any of you at the back who do not hear me, please don't raise your hands because I am also nearsighted.

W. H. AUDEN (1907–73) British poet.
Starting a lecture in a large hall

2 I want to reassure you I am not this size, really – dear me no, I'm being amplified by the mike.

G. K. CHESTERTON (1874–1936) British writer.
At a lecture in Pittsburgh

3 Wery glad to see you indeed, and hope our acquaintance may be a long 'un, as the gen'l'm'n said to the fi' pun' note.

CHARLES DICKENS (1812–70) British novelist.

4 I think it's the most extraordinary collection of talent, of human knowledge, that has ever been gathered together at the White House – with the possible exception of when Thomas Jefferson dined alone.

JOHN FITZGERALD KENNEDY (1917–63) US statesman.
Said at a dinner for Nobel Prizewinners, 29 Apr 1962

5 I want to thank you for stopping the applause. It is impossible for me to look humble for any period of time.

HENRY KISSINGER (1923–) German-born US politician and diplomat.

6 I declare this thing open – whatever it is.

PRINCE PHILIP (1921–) The consort of Queen Elizabeth II.
Opening a new annex at Vancouver City Hall

Quotations About Speeches

How (or how not) to do it

7 Begin low, speak slow; take fire, rise higher; when most impressed be self-possessed; at the end wax warm, and sit down in a storm.

ANONYMOUS

8 This is a rotten argument, but it should be good enough for their lordships on a hot summer afternoon.

ANONYMOUS
A note on a ministerial brief read out by mistake in the House of Lords

9 Let thy speech be short, comprehending much in few words; be as one that knoweth and yet holdeth his tongue.

BIBLE: ECCLESIASTICUS

10 I take the view, and always have done, that if you cannot say what you have to say in twenty minutes, you should go away and write a book about it.

LORD BRABAZON OF TARA (1910–74) British businessman and Conservative politician.

11 Adepts in the speaking trade

Keep a cough by them ready made.

CHARLES CHURCHILL (1731–64) British poet.

12 He is one of those orators of whom it was well said, 'Before they get up they do not know what they are going to say; when they are speaking, they do not know what they are saying; and when they sit down, they do not know what they have said'.

WINSTON CHURCHILL (1874–1965) British statesman. Referring to Lord Charles Beresford

13 A good storyteller is a person who has a good memory and hopes other people haven't.

IRVIN S. COBB (1876–1944) US writer.

14 I dreamt that I was making a speech in the House. I woke up, and by Jove I was!

DUKE OF DEVONSHIRE (1833–1908) Conservative politician.

15 A good indignation makes an excellent speech.

RALPH WALDO EMERSON (1803–82) US poet and essayist.

16 Why doesn't the fellow who says, 'I'm no speech-maker', let it go at that instead of giving a demonstration.

F. McKINNEY HUBBARD (1868–1930) US journalist.

17 A speech is like a love affair: any fool can start one but to end it requires considerable skill.

LORD MANCROFT (1917–87) British businessman and writer.

18 What orators lack in depth they make up to you in length.

BARON DE MONTESQUIEU (1688–1755) French writer.

19 Brevity is the soul of wit.

WILLIAM SHAKESPEARE (1564–1616) English dramatist.

20 For I have neither wit, nor words, nor worth,
Action, nor utterance, nor the power of speech,
To stir men's blood; I only speak right on.

WILLIAM SHAKESPEARE

21 It usually takes more than three weeks to prepare a good impromptu speech.

MARK TWAIN (Samuel Langhorne Clemens; 1835–1910) US writer.

22 Don't quote Latin; say what you have to say, and then sit down.

DUKE OF WELLINGTON (1769–1852) British general and statesman.
Advice to a new Member of Parliament

The Audience

23 If there is anyone here whom I have not insulted, I beg his pardon.

JOHANNES BRAHMS (1833–97) German composer.

24 I always enjoy appearing before a British audience. Even if they don't feel like laughing, they nod their heads to show they've understood.

BOB HOPE (Leslie Townes Hope; 1903–   ) British-born US comedian.

25 I quite agree with you, sir, but what can two do against so many?

GEORGE BERNARD SHAW (1856–1950) Irish dramatist and critic.
Responding to a solitary hiss heard amongst the applause at the first performance of *Arms and the Man* in 1894

26 I would just like to mention Robert Houdin who in the eighteenth century invented the vanishing bird-cage trick and the theater matinée – may he rot and perish. Good afternoon.

ORSON WELLES (1915–85) US film actor.
Addressing the audience at the end of a matinée performance

27 The play was a great success, but the audience was a disaster.

OSCAR WILDE (1854–1900) Irish-born British dramatist.
Referring to a play that had recently failed

QUOTATIONS ABOUT TOPICS

Quotations are given about various topics, which are arranged in alphabetical order.

ABSTINENCE

1 He neither drank, smoked, nor rode a bicycle. Living frugally, saving his money, he died early, surrounded by greedy relatives. It was a great lesson to me.

JOHN BARRYMORE (1882–1942) US actor.

2   Teetotallers lack the sympathy and generosity of men that drink.

W. H. DAVIES (1871–1940) British poet.

3   It was a brilliant affair; water flowed like champagne.

WILLIAM M. EVARTS (1818–1901) US lawyer and statesman.
Describing a dinner given by US President Rutherford B. Hayes (1877–81), an advocate of temperance

4   If you resolve to give up smoking, drinking and loving, you don't actually live longer; it just seems longer.

CLEMENT FREUD (1924–   ) British Liberal politician and broadcaster.

5   Mr Mercaptan went on to preach a brilliant sermon on that melancholy sexual perversion known as continence.

ALDOUS HUXLEY (1894–1964) British novelist.

6   Lastly (and this is, perhaps, the golden rule), no woman should marry a teetotaller, or a man who does not smoke.

ROBERT LOUIS STEVENSON (1850–94) Scottish writer.

ACHIEVEMENT

1   There is no such thing as a great talent without great will-power.

HONORÉ DE BALZAC (1799–1850) French novelist.

2   Genius is one per cent inspiration and ninety-nine per cent perspiration.

THOMAS EDISON (1847–1931) US inventor.

3 Because it is there.

GEORGE MALLORY (1886–1924) British mountaineer.
Answer to the question 'Why do you want to climb Mt. Everest?'

4 For years politicians have promised the moon, I'm the first one to be able to deliver it.

RICHARD MILHOUS NIXON (1913–) US president.

5 A genius! For thirty-seven years I've practiced fourteen hours a day, and now they call me a genius!

PABLO SARASATE (1844–1908) Spanish violinist and composer.
On being hailed as a genius by a critic

6 I did not write it. God wrote it. I merely did his dictation.

HARRIET BEECHER STOWE (1811–96) US novelist.
Referring to *Uncle Tom's Cabin*

7 I started at the top and worked my way down.

ORSON WELLES (1915–85) US film actor.

ADULTERY

1 It is better to be unfaithful than faithful without wanting to be.

BRIGITTE BARDOT (1934–) French film actress.

2 Sara could commit adultery at one end and weep for her sins at the other, and enjoy both operations at once.

JOYCE CARY (1888–1957) British novelist.

3 You know, of course, that the Tasmanians, who never committed adultery, are now extinct.

W. SOMERSET MAUGHAM (1874–1965) British novelist.

4 Madame, you must really be more careful. Suppose it had been someone else who found you like this.

DUC DE RICHELIEU (1766–1822) French statesman.
Discovering his wife with her lover

ADVICE

1 Advice is seldom welcome; and those who want it the most always like it the least.

EARL OF CHESTERFIELD (1694–1773) English statesman.

2 I intended to give you some advice but now I remember how much is left over from last year unused.

GEORGE HARRIS (1844–1922) US congressman.
Said when addressing students at the start of a new academic year

3 No one wants advice – only corroboration.

JOHN STEINBECK (1902–68) US novelist.

4 I have lived some thirty years on this planet, and I have yet to hear the first syllable of valuable or even earnest advice from my seniors.

HENRY DAVID THOREAU (1817–1862) US writer.

AGE

1   Aging seems to be the only available way to live a long time.

DANIEL-FRANÇOIS-ESPRIT AUBER (1782–1871) French composer.

2   The only thing I regret about my past life is the length of it. If I had my past life over again I'd make all the same mistakes – only sooner.

TALLULAH BANKHEAD (1903–68) US actress.

3   What youth deemed crystal, age finds out was dew.

ROBERT BROWNING (1812–89) British poet.

4   I prefer old age to the alternative.

MAURICE CHEVALIER (1888–1972) French singer and actor.

5   Oh to be seventy again.

GEORGES CLEMENCEAU (1841–1929) French statesman. Remark on his eightieth birthday, noticing a pretty girl in the Champs Elysées

6   When a man fell into his anecdotage it was a sign for him to retire from the world.

BENJAMIN DISRAELI (1804–81) British statesman.

7   The years between fifty and seventy are the hardest. You are always being asked to do things, and you are not yet decrepit enough to turn them down.

T. S. ELIOT (1888–1965) US-born British poet and dramatist.

8 At sixteen I was stupid, confused, insecure and indecisive. At twenty-five I was wise, self-confident, prepossessing and assertive. At forty-five I am stupid, confused, insecure and indecisive. Who would have supposed that maturity is only a short break in adolescence?

JULES FEIFFER (1929–   ) US writer, cartoonist, and humorist.

9 He cannot bear old men's jokes. That is not new. But now he begins to think of them himself.

MAX FRISCH (1911–   ) Swiss dramatist and novelist.

10 A diplomat is a man who always remembers a woman's birthday but never remembers her age.

ROBERT FROST (1875–1963) US poet.

11 A man is only as old as the woman he feels.

GROUCHO MARX (Julius Marx; 1895–1977) US comedian.

12 From the earliest times the old have rubbed it into the young that they are wiser than they, and before the young had discovered what nonsense this was they were old too, and it profited them to carry on the imposture.

W. SOMERSET MAUGHAM (1874–1965) British novelist.

13 I prefer to forget both pairs of glasses and pass my declining years saluting strange women and grandfather clocks.

OGDEN NASH (1902–71) US poet.

14 At 50, everyone has the face he deserves.

GEORGE ORWELL (Eric Blair; 1903–50) British novelist. Last words in his manuscript notebook, 17 Apr 1949

15 Each generation imagines itself to be more intelligent than the one that went before it, and wiser than the one that comes after it.

GEORGE ORWELL

16 Growing old is like being increasingly penalized for a crime you haven't committed.

ANTHONY POWELL (1905–   ) British novelist.

17 You know, by the time you reach my age, you've made plenty of mistakes if you've lived your life properly

RONALD REAGAN (1911–   ) US politician and president.

18 The young have aspirations that never come to pass, the old have reminiscences of what never happened.

SAKI (Hector Hugh Munro; 1870–1916) British writer.

19 When I was young, I was told: 'You'll see, when you're fifty.' I am fifty and I haven't seen a thing.

ERIK SATIE (1866–1925) French composer.
From a letter to his brother

20 All that the young can do for the old is to shock them and keep them up to date.

GEORGE BERNARD SHAW (1856–1950) Irish dramatist and critic.

21 It's a funny thing about that bust. As time goes on it seems to get younger and younger.

GEORGE BERNARD SHAW

Referring to a portrait bust sculpted for him by Rodin

22 Old men are dangerous; it doesn't matter to them what is going to happen to the world.

GEORGE BERNARD SHAW

23 If you live long enough, the venerability factor creeps in; you get accused of things you never did and praised for virtues you never had.

I. F. STONE (1907–) US writer and publisher.

24 From birth to age eighteen, a girl needs good parents. From eighteen to thirty-five, she needs good looks. From thirty-five to fifty-five, she needs a good personality. From fifty-five on, she needs good cash.

SOPHIE TUCKER (Sophia Abuza; 1884–1966) Russian-born US singer.

AGREEMENT

1 When you say that you agree to a thing in principle you mean that you have not the slightest intention of carrying it out in practice.

BISMARCK (1815–98) German statesman.

2 Our agenda is now exhausted. The secretary general is exhausted. All of you are exhausted. I find it comforting that, beginning with our very first day, we find ourselves in such complete unanimity.

PAUL HENRI SPAAK (1899–1972) Belgian statesman. Concluding the first General Assembly meeting of the United Nations

3   Ah! don't say you agree with me. When people agree with me I always feel that I must be wrong.

OSCAR WILDE (1854–1900) Irish-born British dramatist.

AMBITION

1   Ah, but a man's reach should exceed his grasp,
Or what's a heaven for?

ROBERT BROWNING (1812–89) British poet.

2   If you would hit the mark, you must aim a little above it;
Every arrow that flies feels the attraction of earth.

HENRY WADSWORTH LONGFELLOW (1807–82) US poet.

3   Fain would I climb, yet fear I to fall.

WALTER RALEIGH (1554–1618) English explorer.
Written on a window pane with his diamond ring. He was alluding to his relationship with Queen Elizabeth I, who wrote a reply underneath, 'If thy heart fails thee, climb not at all'.

4   Ambition often puts Men upon doing the meanest offices; so climbing is performed in the same position with creeping.

JONATHAN SWIFT (1667–1745) Irish-born Anglican priest and writer.

5   There is always room at the top.

DANIEL WEBSTER (1782–1852) US statesman.
When advised not to become a lawyer because the profession was overcrowded

ANIMALS

1   I know two things about the horse,
    And one of them is rather coarse.

    ANONYMOUS

2   It takes a good deal of physical courage to ride a
    horse. This, however, I have. I get it at about forty
    cents a flask, and take it as required.

    STEPHEN LEACOCK (1869–1944) English-born Canadian
    economist and humorist.

3   To confess that you are totally Ignorant about the
    Horse, is social suicide: you will be despised by
    everybody, especially the horse.

    W. C. SELLAR (1898–1951) British humorous writer.

4   Nowadays we don't think much of a man's love for
    an animal; we laugh at people who are attached to
    cats. But if we stop loving animals, aren't we bound
    to stop loving humans too?

    ALEXANDER SOLZHENITSYN (1918–   ) Soviet novelist.

5   There are two things for which animals are to be
    envied: they know nothing of future evils, or of what
    people say about them.

    VOLTAIRE (François-Marie Arouet; 1694–1778) French
    writer.

APOLOGIES

1   Very sorry can't come. Lie follows by post.

    CHARLES BERESFORD (1846–1919) British naval officer.

Reply, by telegram, to a dinner invitation at short notice from Edward, Prince of Wales

2   Mr. Speaker, I said the honorable member was a liar it is true and I am sorry for it. The honourable member may place the punctuation where he pleases.

RICHARD BRINSLEY SHERIDAN (1751–1816) British dramatist.
On being asked to apologize for calling a fellow MP a liar

3   It is a good rule in life never to apologize. The right sort of people do not want apologies, and the wrong sort take a mean advantage of them.

P. G. WODEHOUSE (1881–1975) British humorous novelist.

APPEARANCE

1   It was a blonde. A blonde to make a bishop kick a hole in a stained-glass window.

RAYMOND CHANDLER (1888–1959) US novelist.

2   The most delightful advantage of being bald – one can hear snowflakes.

R. G. DANIELS (1916–   ) British magistrate.

3   I am so changed that my oldest creditors would hardly know me.

HENRY STEPHEN FOX (1791–1846) British diplomat.
Remark after an illness

4   To see ourselves as others see us is a most salutary
     gift. Hardly less important is the capacity to see
     others as they see themselves.

     ALDOUS HUXLEY (1894–1964) British novelist.

5   The Lord prefers common-looking people. That is
     why he makes so many of them.

     ABRAHAM LINCOLN (1809–65) US statesman.

6   He looks as if he had been weaned on a pickle.

     ALICE ROOSEVELT LONGWORTH (1884–1980) US hostess.
     Referring to John Calvin Coolidge, US president 1923–29

ARGUMENTS

1   Between friends differences in taste or opinion are
     irritating in direct proportion to their triviality.

     W. H. AUDEN (1907–73) British poet.

2   Never go to bed mad. Stay up and fight.

     PHYLLIS DILLER (1917–74) US writer and comedienne.

3   One often contradicts an opinion when what is un-
     congenial is really the tone in which it was
     conveyed.

     FRIEDRICH WILHELM NIETZSCHE (1844–1900) German
     philosopher.

4   A man never tells you anything until you contradict
     him.

     GEORGE BERNARD SHAW (1856–1950) Irish dramatist and
     critic.

5   I did not know that we had ever quarrelled.

HENRY DAVID THOREAU (1817–62) US writer.
On being urged to make his peace with God

6   Arguments are to be avoided: they are always vulgar and often unconvincing.

OSCAR WILDE (1854–1900) Irish-born British dramatist.

ART

1   The object of art is to give life a shape.

JEAN ANOUILH (1910–87) French dramatist

2   Remember I'm an artist. And you know what that means in a court of law. Next worst to an actress.

JOYCE CARY (1888–1957) British novelist

3   Buy old masters. They fetch a better price than old mistresses.

LORD BEAVERBROOK (1879–1964) Canadian-born British newspaper proprietor.

4   Art is a jealous mistress.

RALPH WALDO EMERSON (1803–82) US poet and essayist.

5   The finest collection of frames I ever saw.

HUMPHRY DAVY (1778–1829) British chemist.
When asked what he thought of the Paris art galleries

6   The trouble, Mr Goldwyn is that you are only interested in art and I am only interested in money.

GEORGE BERNARD SHAW (1856–1950) Irish dramatist and critic.

Turning down Goldwyn's offer to buy the screen rights of his plays

7 Skill without imagination is craftsmanship and gives us many useful objects such as wickerwork picnic baskets. Imagination without skill gives us modern art.

TOM STOPPARD (1937–) Czech-born British dramatist

AWARDS

1 I don't deserve this, but I have arthritis, and I don't deserve that either.

JACK BENNY (Benjamin Kubelsky; 1894–1974) US actor. Said when accepting an award

2 When I want a peerage, I shall buy one like an honest man.

LORD NORTHCLIFFE (1865–1922) Irish-born British newspaper proprietor.

3 Mother always told me my day was coming, but I never realized that I'd end up being the shortest knight of the year.

GORDON RICHARDS (1904–86) British champion jockey. Referring to his diminutive size, on hearing he had been awarded a knighthood

BEAUTY

1 A thing of beauty is a joy for ever:
Its loveliness increases; it will never
Pass into nothingness; but still will keep
A bower quiet for us, and a sleep

Full of sweet dreams, and health, and quiet breathing.

JOHN KEATS (1795–1821) British poet.

2　'Beauty is truth, truth beauty,' – that is all
Ye know on earth, and all ye need to know.

JOHN KEATS

3　Oh, thou art fairer than the evening air
Clad in the beauty of a thousand stars.

CHRISTOPHER MARLOWE (1564–93) English dramatist.

4　Remember that the most beautiful things in the world are the most useless, peacocks and lilies for instance.

JOHN RUSKIN (1819–1900) British art critic and writer.

5　I always say beauty is only sin deep.

SAKI (Hector Hugh Munro; 1870–1916) British writer.

BEGINNING

1　The distance doesn't matter; it is only the first step that is difficult.

MARQUISE DU DEFFAND (Marie de Vichy-Chamrond; 1697–1780) French noblewoman.
Referring to the legend of St Denis, who is traditionally believed to have carried his severed head for six miles after his execution

2　'Tis always morning somewhere in the world.

RICHARD HENRY HORNE (1803–84) English writer.

BETRAYAL

1   I hate the idea of causes, and if I had to choose be-
    tween betraying my country and betraying my
    friend, I hope I should have the guts to betray my
    country.

    E. M. FORSTER (1879–1970) British novelist.

2   Treason doth never prosper: what's the reason?
    For if it prosper, none dare call it treason.

    JOHN HARINGTON (1561–1612) English writer.

3   I'm waiting for the cock to crow.

    WILLIAM MORRIS HUGHES (1864–1952) Australian
    statesman.
    Said in parliament, after being viciously critized by a
    member of his own party

BOASTS

1   To give an accurate and exhaustive account of that
    period would need a far less brilliant pen than mine.

    MAX BEERBOHM (1872–1956) British writer.

2   I have done almost every human activity inside a
    taxi which does not require main drainage.

    ALAN BRIEN (1925–   ) British critic.

3   All my shows are great. Some of them are bad. But
    they are all great.

    LEW GRADE (Lewis Winogradsky; 1906–   ) British film
    and TV producer.

4   I can piss the old boy in the snow.

MAX LIEBERMANN (1847–1935) German painter.
Remark to an artist who said he could not draw General
Paul von Hindenburg's face

5 I cannot tell you that, madam. Heaven has granted
me no offspring.

JAMES WHISTLER (1834–1903) US painter.
Replying to a lady who had inquired whether he thought
genius hereditary

6 Nothing, except my genius.

OSCAR WILDE (1854–1900) Irish-born British dramatist.
Replying to a US customs official on being asked if he
had anything to declare

7 Who am I to tamper with a masterpiece?

OSCAR WILDE
Refusing to make alterations to one of his own plays

8 And when we open our dykes, the waters are ten
feet deep.

WILHELMINA (1880–1962) Queen of the Netherlands.
Replying to a boast by Wilhelm II that his guardsmen
were all seven feet tall

BOOKS

1 And further, by these, my son, be admonished: of
making many books there is no end; and much study
is a weariness of the flesh.

BIBLE: ECCLESIASTES

2 A good book is the purest essence of a human soul.

THOMAS CARLYLE (1795–1881) Scottish historian and
essayist.

Speech made in support of the London Library

3   Learning hath gained most by those books by which the printers have lost.

THOMAS FULLER (1608–61) English historian.

4   A book may be amusing with numerous errors, or it may be very dull without a single absurdity.

OLIVER GOLDSMITH (1728–74) Irish-born British writer.

B U R E A U C R A C Y

1   A memorandum is written not to inform the reader but to protect the writer.

DEAN ACHESON (1893–1971) US lawyer and statesman.

2   I'm surprised that a government organization could do it that quickly.

JIMMY CARTER (1924–) US statesman.
Visiting Egypt, when told that it took twenty years to build the Great Pyramid

3   A committee is a cul-de-sac down which ideas are lured and then quietly strangled.

BARNETT COCKS (1907–) British political writer.

4   The number one book of the ages was written by a committee, and it was called The Bible.

LOUIS B. MAYER (1885–1957) Russian-born US film producer.
Comment to writers who had objected to changes in their work

BUSINESS

1   You ask me what it is I do. Well actually, you know,
I'm partly a liaison man and partly P.R.O.
Essentially I integrate the current export drive
And basically I'm viable from ten o'clock till five.

JOHN BETJEMAN (1906–84) British poet.

2   Here's the rule for bargains: 'Do other men, for
they would do you'. That's the true business
precept.

CHARLES DICKENS (1812–70) British novelist.

3   No nation was ever ruined by trade.

BENJAMIN FRANKLIN (1706–90) US scientist and
statesman.

4   The salary of the chief executive of the large corpo-
ration is not a market award for achievement. It is
frequently in the nature of a warm personal gesture
by the individual to himself.

JOHN KENNETH GALBRAITH (1908–) US economist.

5   Where wealth and freedom reign, contentment fails
And honour sinks where commerce long prevails.

OLIVER GOLDSMITH (1728–74) Irish-born British writer.

6   When you are skinning your customers, you should
leave some skin on to grow so that you can skin
them again.

NIKITA KHRUSHCHEV (1894–1971) Soviet statesman.
Said to British businessmen

7   He is the only man who is for ever apologizing for
his occupation.

H. L. MENCKEN (1880–1956) US journalist.
Referring to the businessman

8 The big print giveth and the fine print taketh away.

J. FULTON SHEEN (1895–1979) US Roman Catholic
archbishop.
Referring to his contract for a television appearance

9 People of the same trade seldom meet together but
the conversation ends in a conspiracy against the
public, or in some diversion to raise prices.

ADAM SMITH (1723–90) Scottish economist.

10 You never expected justice from a company, did
you? They have neither a soul to lose nor a body to
kick.

SYDNEY SMITH (1771–1845) British clergyman and
essayist.

11 All business sagacity reduces itself in the last analy-
sis to a judicious use of sabotage.

THORSTEIN BUNDE VEBLEN (1857–1929) US social
scientist.

12 If Max gets to Heaven he won't last long. He will be
chucked out for trying to pull off a merger between
Heaven and Hell . . . after having secured a control-
ling interest in key subsidiary companies in both
places, of course.

H. G. WELLS (1866–1946) British writer.
Referring to Lord Beaverbrook

13 Business underlies everything in our national life, including our spiritual life. Witness the fact that in the
Lord's Prayer the first petition is for daily bread. No
one can worship God or love his neighbour on an
empty stomach.

WOODROW WILSON (1856–1925) US statesman.

CENSORSHIP

1 Whenever books are burned men also in the end are
burned.

HEINRICH HEINE (1797–1856) German poet and writer.

2 Censorship is more depraving and corrupting than
anything pornography can produce.

TONY SMYTHE (1938–   ) Chairman of the National
Council for Civil Liberties, Great Britain.

3 God forbid that any book should be banned. The
practice is as indefensible as infanticide.

REBECCA WEST (Cicely Isabel Fairfield; 1892–1983)
British novelist and journalist.

CHANCE

1 When you take the bull by the horns . . . what happens is a toss up.

WILLIAM PETT RIDGE (1860–1930) British novelist.

CHARACTER

1 It is with narrow-souled people as with narrow-necked bottles: the less they have in them, the more noise they make in pouring it out.

ALEXANDER POPE (1688–1744) British poet.

CHARITY

1 Don't bother to thank me. I know what a perfectly ghastly season it's been for you Spanish dancers.

TALLULAH BANKHEAD (1903–68) US actress.
Said on dropping fifty dollars into a tambourine held out by a Salvation Army collector

2 If you see anybody fallen by the wayside and lying in the ditch, it isn't much good climbing into the ditch and lying by his side.

H. R. L. SHEPPARD (1880–1937) British clergyman.

3 To keep a lamp burning we have to keep putting oil in it.

MOTHER TERESA (Agnes Gonxha Bojaxhui; 1910– ·)
Yugoslavian missionary in Calcutta.

CHARM

1 It's a sort of bloom on a woman. If you have it, you don't need to have anything else; and if you don't have it, it doesn't much matter what else you have.

J. M. BARRIE (1860–1937) British novelist and dramatist.

CHILDREN

1   Children have never been very good at listening to their elders, but they have never failed to imitate them.

JAMES BALDWIN (1924–87) US writer.

2   A woman when she is in travail hath sorrow, because her hour is come: but as soon as she is delivered of the child, she remembereth no more the anguish, for joy that a man is born into the world.

BIBLE: JOHN

3   Boys do not grow up gradually. They move forward in spurts like the hands of clocks in railway stations.

CYRIL CONNOLLY (1903–74) British journalist.

4   If men had to have babies they would only ever have one each.

DIANA, PRINCESS OF WALES (1961–   ) Wife of Prince Charles.

5   Every baby born into the world is a finer one than the last.

CHARLES DICKENS (1812–70) British novelist.

6   It is only rarely that one can see in a little boy the promise of a man, but one can almost always see in a little girl the threat of a woman.

ALEXANDRE DUMAS, FILS (1824–95) French writer.

7   A loud noise at one end and no sense of responsibility at the other.

RONALD KNOX (1888–1957) British Roman Catholic priest.

8 The baby doesn't understand English and the Devil knows Latin.

RONALD KNOX
Said when asked to conduct a baptism service in English

9 Death and taxes and childbirth! There's never any convenient time for any of them!

MARGARET MITCHELL (1909–49) US novelist.

10 Dear Mary, We all knew you had it in you.

DOROTHY PARKER (1893–1967) US writer.

11 He that has no children brings them up well.

PROVERB

12 There's only one pretty child in the world, and every mother has it.

PROVERB

13 Parents learn a lot from their children about coping with life.

MURIEL SPARK (1918–) British novelist.

14 Never have children, only grandchildren.

GORE VIDAL (1925–) US novelist.

CHIVALRY

1 A gentleman is any man who wouldn't hit a woman with his hat on.

FRED ALLEN (1894–1956) US comedian.

2 Madame, I would have given you another!

ALFRED JARRY (1873–1907) French surrealist dramatist.
On being reprimanded by a woman for firing his pistol in
the vicinity of her child, who might have been killed

CIVILIZATION

1 Civilization is a method of living, an attitude of equal
respect for all men.

JANE ADDAMS (1860–1935) US social worker.

2 I think it would be a good idea.

MAHATMA GANDHI (Mohandas Karamchand Gandhi;
1869–1948) Indian national leader.
On being asked for his view on Western civilization

3 The degree of a nation's civilization is marked by its
disregard for the necessities of existence.

W. SOMERSET MAUGHAM (1874–1965) British novelist.

CLOTHES

1 I go to a better tailor than any of you and pay more
for my clothes. The only difference is that you probably don't sleep in yours.

CLARENCE SEWARD DARROW (1857–1938) US lawyer.

Reply when teased by reporters about his appearance

2 How do you look when I'm sober?

RING LARDNER JNR (1885–1933) American humorist.
Speaking to a flamboyantly dressed stranger who walked
into the club where he was drinking

3 Brevity is the soul of lingerie.

DOROTHY PARKER (1893–1967) US writer.

COMMUNISM

1 Communism is like prohibition, it's a good idea but it
won't work.

WILL ROGERS (1879–1935) US actor and humorist.

COMPLAINTS

1 I want to register a complaint. Do you know who
sneaked into my room at three o'clock this morning?
. . .
– Who? . . .
Nobody, and that's my complaint.

GROUCHO MARX (Julius Marx; 1895–1977) US
comedian.

2 If this is the way Queen Victoria treats her prisoners, she doesn't deserve to have any.

OSCAR WILDE (1854–1900 Irish-born British dramatist.
Complaining at having to wait in the rain for transport to
take him to prison

COMPLIMENTS

1   She walks in beauty, like the night
    Of cloudless climes and starry skies;
    And all that's best of dark and bright
    Meet in her aspect and her eyes.

    LORD BYRON (1788–1824) British poet.

2   Your eyes shine like the pants of my blue serge suit.

    GROUCHO MARX (Julius Marx; 1895–1977) US
    comedian.

3   Age cannot wither her, nor custom stale
    Her infinite variety. Other women cloy
    The appetites they feed, but she makes hungry
    Where most she satisfies.

    WILLIAM SHAKESPEARE (1564–1616) English dramatist.

4   'A was a man, take him for all in all,
    I shall not look upon his like again.

    WILLIAM SHAKESPEARE

5   Shall I compare thee to a summer's day?
    Thou art more lovely and more temperate.
    Rough winds do shake the darling buds of May,
    And summer's lease hath all too short a date.

    WILLIAM SHAKESPEARE

6   Won't you come into the garden? I would like my
    roses to see you.

    RICHARD BRINSLEY SHERIDAN (1751–1816) British
    dramatist.
    Said to a young lady

7   She would rather light candles than curse the darkness, and her glow has warmed the world.

ADLAI STEVENSON (1900–65) US statesman.
Referring to Eleanor Roosevelt

8   What, when drunk, one sees in other women, one sees in Garbo sober.

KENNETH TYNAN (1927–80) British theatre critic.

9   He was a great patriot, a humanitarian, a loyal friend – provided, of course, that he really is dead.

VOLTAIRE (François-Marie Arouet; 1694–1778) French writer.
Giving a funeral oration

COMPROMISE

1   You cannot shake hands with a clenched fist.

INDIRA GANDHI (1917–84) Indian stateswoman.

CONCEIT

1   No poet or novelist wishes he were the only one who ever lived, but most of them wish they were the only one alive, and quite a number fondly believe their wish has been granted.

W. H. AUDEN (1907–73) British poet.

2   *Egotist,* n. A person of low taste, more interested in himself than in me.

AMBROSE BIERCE (1842–?1914) US writer and journalist.

3   I know he is, and he adores his maker.

>   BENJAMIN DISRAELI (1804–81) British statesman.
>   Replying to a remark made in defence of John Bright
>   that he was a self-made man; often also attrib. to Bright
>   referring to Disraeli

CONTRACEPTION

1   I want to tell you a terrific story about oral contraception. I asked this girl to sleep with me and she said 'no'.

>   WOODY ALLEN (Allen Stewart Konigsberg; 1935–)
>   US film actor.

2   Contraceptives should be used on every conceivable occasion.

>   SPIKE MILLIGAN (1918–) British comic actor and author.

COURAGE

1   Because of my title, I was the first to enter here. I shall be the last to go out.

>   DUCHESSE D'ALENÇON (d. 1897) Bavarian-born duchess.
>   Refusing help during a fire, 4 May 1897, at a charity bazaar in Paris. She died along with 120 others.

2   If the creator had a purpose in equipping us with a neck, he surely meant us to stick it out.

>   ARTHUR KOESTLER (1905–83) Hungarian-born British writer.

3   Let me assert my firm belief that the only thing we have to fear is fear itself.

FRANKLIN D. ROOSEVELT (1882–1945) US Democratic president.

4 He was a bold man that first eat an oyster.

JONATHAN SWIFT (1667–1745) Irish-born Anglican priest and writer.

CRITICISM

1 There is less in this than meets the eye.

TALLULAH BANKHEAD (1903–68) US actress.
Referring to a revival of a play by Maeterlinck

2 He played the King as though under momentary apprehension that someone else was about to play the ace.

EUGENE FIELD (1850–95) US poet and journalist.
Referring to Creston Clarke's performance in the role of King Lear

3 My dear chap! Good isn't the word!

W. S. GILBERT (1836–1911) British dramatist.
Speaking to an actor after he had given a poor performance

4 We were as nearly bored as enthusiasm would permit.

EDMUND GOSSE (1849–1928) British writer and critic.
Referring to a play by Swinburne

5 Difficult do you call it, Sir? I wish it were impossible.

SAMUEL JOHNSON (1709–84) British lexicographer.
On hearing a famous violinist and being told that the piece played was difficult

6 A fly, Sir, may sting a stately horse and make him wince; but one is but an insect, and the other is a horse still.

SAMUEL JOHNSON

7 From the moment I picked up your book until I laid it down, I was convulsed with laughter. Some day I intend reading it.

GROUCHO MARX (Julius Marx; 1895–1977) US comedian and film actor.

8 Your works will be read after Shakespeare and Milton are forgotten – and not till then.

RICHARD PORSON (1759–1808) British classicist.
Giving his opinion of the poems of Robert Southey

9 It had only one fault. It was kind of lousy.

JAMES THURBER (1894–1961) US humorist.
Remark made about a play

10 I do not think this poem will reach its destination.

VOLTAIRE (François-Marie Arouet; 1694–1778) French writer.
Reviewing Rousseau's poem 'Ode to Posterity'

11 My dear fellow a unique evening! I wouldn't have left a turn unstoned.

ARTHUR WIMPERIS (1874–1953) British screenwriter.
Replying when asked his opinion of a vaudeville show

12 I saw it at a disadvantage – the curtain was up.

WALTER WINCHELL (1879–1972) US journalist.
Referring to a show starring Earl Carroll

CYNICISM

1   One is not superior merely because one sees the world in an odious light.

    VICOMTE DE CHATEAUBRIAND (1768–1848) French diplomat and writer.

2   A man who knows the price of everything and the value of nothing.

    OSCAR WILDE (1854–1900) Irish-born British dramatist.

DEATH

1   It's not that I'm afraid to die. I just don't want to be there when it happens.

    WOODY ALLEN (Allen Stewart Konigsberg; 1935–   )
    US film actor.

2   I don't want to achieve immortality through my work . . . I want to achieve it through not dying.

    WOODY ALLEN

3   I have often thought upon death, and I find it the least of all evils.

    FRANCIS BACON (1561–1626) English philosopher.

4   It is important what a man still plans at the end. It shows the measure of injustice in his death.

    ELIAS CANETTI (1905–   ) Bulgarian-born novelist.

5   It matters not how a man dies, but how he lives. The act of dying is not of importance, it lasts so short a time.

SAMUEL JOHNSON (1709–84) British lexicographer.

6   That is the road we all have to take – over the Bridge of Sighs into eternity.

SØREN KIERKEGAARD (1813–55) Danish philosopher.

7   Dying is a very dull, dreary affair. And my advice to you is to have nothing whatever to do with it.

W. SOMERSET MAUGHAM (1874–1965) British novelist.

8   Sleep after toil, port after stormy seas,
Ease after war, death after life does greatly please.

EDMUND SPENSER (1552–99) English poet.

DEBAUCHERY

1   A great many people have come up to me and asked how I manage to get so much work done and still keep looking so dissipated.

ROBERT BENCHLEY (1889–1945) US humorist.

2   Once: a philosopher; twice: a pervert!

VOLTAIRE (François-Marie Arouet; 1694–1778) French writer.
Turning down an invitation to an orgy, having attended one the previous night for the first time

DECEPTION

1   Beware of false prophets, which come to you in sheep's clothing, but inwardly they are ravening wolves.

BIBLE: MATTHEW

2   You can fool some of the people all the time and all the people some of the time; but you can't fool all the people all the time.

ABRAHAM LINCOLN (1809–65) US statesman.

3   You can fool too many of the people too much of the time.

JAMES THURBER (1894–1961) US humorist.

DEMOCRACY

1   Democracy means government by discussion but it is only effective if you can stop people talking.

CLEMENT ATTLEE (1883–1967) British statesman and Labour prime minister.

2   Democracy means government by the uneducated, while aristocracy means government by the badly educated.

G. K. CHESTERTON (1874–1936) British writer.

3   It's not the voting that's democracy; it's the counting.

TOM STOPPARD (1937–) Czech-born British dramatist.

DESTINY

1   The Moving Finger writes; and, having writ,
Moves on: nor all thy Piety nor Wit
Shall lure it back to cancel half a Line,
Nor all thy Tears wash out a Word of it.

EDWARD FITZGERALD (1809–83) British poet.

DIPLOMACY

1   It is better for aged diplomats to be bored than for young men to die.

    WARREN AUSTIN   (1877–1962)   US politician and diplomat. When asked if he got tired during long debates at the UN

2   An appeaser is one who feeds a crocodile – hoping that it will eat him last.

    WINSTON CHURCHILL   (1874–1965)   British statesman.

3   A diplomat these days is nothing but a head-waiter who's allowed to sit down occasionally.

    PETER USTINOV   (1921–   )   British actor

4   An ambassador is an honest man sent to lie abroad for the good of his country.

    HENRY WOTTON   (1568–1639)   English poet and diplomat.

DOGS

1   The great pleasure of a dog is that you may make a fool of yourself with him and not only will he not scold you, he will make a fool of himself too.

    SAMUEL BUTLER   (1835–1902)   British writer.

2   A door is what a dog is perpetually on the wrong side of.

    OGDEN NASH   (1902–71)   US poet.

3   I loathe people who keep dogs. They are cowards who haven't got the guts to bite people themselves.

AUGUST STRINDBERG (1849–1912) Swedish dramatist.

DOUBT

1   The trouble with the world is that the stupid are cocksure and the intelligent full of doubt.

BERTRAND RUSSELL (1872–1970) British philosopher.

DRINKING

1   If all be true that I do think,
There are five reasons we should drink;
Good wine – a friend – or being dry –
Or lest we should be by and by –
Or any other reason why.

DEAN ALDRICH (1647–1710) English poet.

2   One reason I don't drink is that I want to know when I am having a good time.

NANCY ASTOR (1879–1964) American-born British politician.

3   So who's in a hurry?

ROBERT BENCHLEY (1889–1945) US humorist.
When asked whether he knew that drinking was a slow death

4   Drink no longer water, but use a little wine for thy stomach's sake and thine often infirmities.

BIBLE: I TIMOTHY

5   Alcohol is like love: the first kiss is magic, the second is intimate, the third is routine. After that you just take the girl's clothes off.

RAYMOND CHANDLER (1888–1959) US novelist.

6   If you believe Cratinus from days of old, Maecenas, (as you must know) no verse can give pleasure for long, nor last, that is written by drinkers of water.

HORACE (Quintus Horatius Flaccus; 65–8 BC) Roman poet.

7   Malt does more than Milton can
To justify God's ways to man.

A. E. HOUSMAN (1859–1936) British scholar and poet.

8   A tavern chair is the throne of human felicity.

SAMUEL JOHNSON (1709–84) British lexicographer.

9   There is nothing which has yet been contrived by man, by which so much happiness is produced as by a good tavern or inn.

SAMUEL JOHNSON

10   Even though a number of people have tried, no one has yet found a way to drink for a living.

JEAN KERR (1923–   ) US dramatist.

11   I drink for the thirst to come.

FRANÇOIS RABELAIS (1483–1553) French satirist.

12   I am as drunk as a lord, but then, I am one, so what does it matter?

BERTRAND RUSSELL (1872–1970) British philosopher.

13   People may say what they like about the decay of Christianity; the religious system that produced green Chartreuse can never really die.

SAKI (Hector Hugh Munro; 1870–1916) British writer.

14 It provokes the desire, but it takes away the performance. Therefore much drink may be said to be an equivocator with lechery.

WILLIAM SHAKESPEARE (1564–1616) English dramatist.

15 Alcohol is a very necessary article . . . It enables Parliament to do things at eleven at night that no sane person would do at eleven in the morning.

GEORGE BERNARD SHAW (1856–1950) Irish dramatist and critic.

16 I hadn't the heart to touch my breakfast. I told Jeeves to drink it himself.

P. G. WODEHOUSE (1881–1975) British humorous novelist.

ECONOMICS

1 Recession is when a neighbour loses his job; depression is when you lose yours.

RONALD REAGAN (1911–   ) US politician and president.

2 If all economists were laid end to end, they would not reach a conclusion.

GEORGE BERNARD SHAW (1856–1950) Irish dramatist and critic.

3 Give me a one-handed economist! All my economists say, 'on the one hand . . . on the other'.

HARRY S. TRUMAN (1884–1972)

EDUCATION

1   Miss not the discourse of the elders: for they also learned of their fathers, and of them thou shalt learn understanding, and to give answer as need requireth.

BIBLE: ECCLESIASTICUS

2   *Brain*, n. An apparatus with which we think that we think.

AMBROSE BIERCE (1842–?1914) US writer and journalist.

3   Education is simply the soul of a society as it passes from one generation to another.

G. K. CHESTERTON (1874–1936) British writer.

4   Examinations are formidable even to the best pre-pared, for the greatest fool may ask more than the wisest man can answer.

CHARLES CALEB COLTON (?1780–1832) British clergy-man and writer.

5   We know the human brain is a device to keep the ears from grating on one another.

PETER DE VRIES (1910–) US novelist.

6   When a man's education is finished, he is finished.

E. A. FILENE (1860–1937) US financier.

7   Spoon feeding in the long run teaches us nothing but the shape of the spoon.

E. M. FORSTER (1879–1970) British novelist.

8   ... that is what learning is. You suddenly understand something you've understood all your life, but
in a new way.

DORIS LESSING (1919–   ) British novelist.

9   A man who has never gone to school may steal from
a freight car, but if he has a university education he
may steal the whole railroad.

FRANKLIN D. ROOSEVELT (1882–1945) US Democratic
president.

10 There is nothing on earth intended for innocent people so horrible as a school. It is in some respects
more cruel than a prison. In a prison, for example,
you are not forced to read books written by the
warders and the governor.

GEORGE BERNARD SHAW (1856–1950) Irish dramatist
and critic.

11 I have never let my schooling interfere with my
education.

MARK TWAIN (Samuel Langhorne Clemens; 1835–1910)
US writer.

12 Anyone who has been to an English public school
will always feel comparatively at home in prison.

EVELYN WAUGH (1903–66) British novelist.

13 Education is an admirable thing, but it is well to remember from time to time that nothing that is worth
knowing can be taught.

OSCAR WILDE (1854–1900) Irish-born British dramatist.

ENDURANCE

1   ... we could never learn to be brave and patient, if there were only joy in the world.

HELEN KELLER (1880–1968) US writer and lecturer.

2   No pain, no palm; no thorns, no throne; no gall, no glory; no cross, no crown.

WILLIAM PENN (1644–1718) English preacher.

3   The pain passes, but the beauty remains.

PIERRE AUGUSTE RENOIR (1841–1919) French impressionist painter.
Explaining why he still painted when his hands were twisted with arthritis

4   Does the road wind up-hill all the way?
Yes, to the very end.
Will the day's journey take the whole long day?
From morn to night, my friend.

CHRISTINA ROSSETTI (1830–74) British poet.

5   For there was never yet philosopher
That could endure the toothache patiently.

WILLIAM SHAKESPEARE (1564–1616) English dramatist.

6   Maybe one day we shall be glad to remember even these hardships.

VIRGIL (Publius Vergilius Maro; 70–19 BC) Roman poet.

ENEMIES

1   Even a paranoid can have enemies.

HENRY KISSINGER (1923–) German-born US politician
and diplomat.

2   It takes your enemy and your friend, working together, to hurt you to the heart; the one to slander
you and the other to get the news to you.

MARK TWAIN (Samuel Langhorne Clemens; 1835–1910)
US writer.

ENTHUSIASM

1   Nothing great was ever achieved without
enthusiasm.

RALPH WALDO EMERSON (1803–82) US poet and
essayist.

ENVY

1   The man with toothache thinks everyone happy
whose teeth are sound.

GEORGE BERNARD SHAW (1856–1950) Irish dramatist
and critic.

EQUALITY

1   The majestic egalitarianism of the law, which forbids
rich and poor alike to sleep under bridges, to beg in
the streets, and to steal bread.

ANATOLE FRANCE (Jacques Anatole François Thibault;
1844–1924) French writer.

2   Your levellers wish to level *down* as far as them-
     selves; but they cannot bear levelling *up* to
     themselves.

     SAMUEL JOHNSON (1709–84) British lexicographer.

3   In heaven an angel is nobody in particular.

     GEORGE BERNARD SHAW (1856–1950) Irish dramatist
     and critic.

4   Everybody should have an equal chance – but they
     shouldn't have a flying start.

     HAROLD WILSON (1916–   ) British politician and prime
     minister.

EXCESS

1   In baiting a mouse-trap with cheese, always leave
     room for the mouse.

     SAKI (Hector Hugh Munro; 1870–1916) British writer.

2   Moderation is a fatal thing, Lady Hunstanton. Noth-
     ing succeeds like excess.

     OSCAR WILDE (1854–1900) Irish-born British dramatist.

EXCUSES

1   Nothing grows well in the shade of a big tree.

     CONSTANTIN BRANCUSI (1876–1957) Romanian sculptor.
     Refusing Rodin's invitation to work in his studio

2   Thank you for the manuscript; I shall lose no time in
     reading it.

     BENJAMIN DISRAELI (1804–81) British statesman.

His customary reply to those who sent him unsolicited manuscripts

3   When a stupid man is doing something he is ashamed of, he always declares that it is his duty.

GEORGE BERNARD SHAW (1856–1950) Irish dramatist and critic.

EXPERIENCE

1   One should try everything once, except incest and folk-dancing.

ARNOLD BAX (1883–1953) British composer.

EXPERTS

1   An expert is a man who has made all the mistakes, which can be made, in a very narrow field.

NIELS BOHR (1885–1962) Danish physicist.

2   Specialist – A man who knows more and more about less and less.

WILLIAM JAMES MAYO (1861–1934) US surgeon.

FAILURE

1   The best laid schemes o' mice an' men
    Gang aft a-gley,
    An' lea'e us nought but grief an' pain
    For promis'd joy.

ROBERT BURNS (1759–96) Scottish poet.

2 He said that he was too old to cry, but it hurt too much to laugh.

ADLAI STEVENSON (1900–65) US statesman.
Said after losing an election, quoting a story told by Abraham Lincoln

3 Well, I have one consolation, No candidate was ever elected ex-president by such a large majority!

WILLIAM HOWARD TAFT (1857–1930) US statesman.
Referring to his disastrous defeat in the 1912 presidential election

---

FAITH

1 I feel no need for any other faith than my faith in human beings.

PEARL BUCK (1892–1973) US novelist.

2 My dear child, you must believe in God in spite of what the clergy tell you.

BENJAMIN JOWETT (1817–93) British theologian.

3 'Tis not the dying for a faith that's so hard, Master Harry – every man of every nation has done that – 'tis the living up to it that is difficult.

WILLIAM MAKEPEACE THACKERAY (1811–63) British novelist.

FAME

1 A celebrity is a person who works hard all his life to become known, then wears dark glasses to avoid being recognized.

FRED ALLEN (1894–1956) US comedian.

2   Being a star has made it possible for me to get insulted in places where the average Negro could never hope to get insulted.

SAMMY DAVIS JNR (1925–   ) Black US singer.

3   If you have to tell them who you are, you aren't anybody.

GREGORY PECK (1916–   ) US film star.
Remarking upon the failure of anyone in a crowded restaurant to recognize him

4   Wealth is like sea-water; the more we drink, the thirstier we become; and the same is true of fame.

ARTHUR SCHOPENHAUER (1788–1860) German philosopher.

FAMILY

1   If one is not going to take the necessary precautions to avoid having parents one must undertake to bring them up.

QUENTIN CRISP (1910–   ) British model, publicist, and writer.

2   Keeping up with the Joneses was a full-time job with my mother and father. It was not until many years later when I lived alone that I realized how much cheaper it was to drag the Joneses down to my level.

QUENTIN CRISP

3   Fate chooses your relations, you choose your friends.

Jacques Delille (1738–1813) French abbé and poet.

4   You're a disgrace to our family name of Wagstaff, if such a thing is possible.

Groucho Marx (Julius Marx; 1895–1977) US comedian.

5   No matter how many communes anybody invents, the family always creeps back.

Margaret Mead (1901–78) US anthropologist.

6   Parents are sometimes a bit of a disappointment to their children. They don't fulfil the promise of their early years.

Anthony Powell (1905–   ) British novelist.

7   It is a wise father that knows his own child.

William Shakespeare (1564–1616) English dramatist.

8   No man is responsible for his father. That is entirely his mother's affair.

Margaret Turnbull (fl. 1920s–1942) US writer.

9   Don't hold your parents up to contempt. After all, you are their son, and it is just possible that you may take after them.

Evelyn Waugh (1903–66) British novelist.

10   The thing that impresses me most about America is the way parents obey their children.

Duke of Windsor (1894–1972) King of the United Kingdom; abdicated 1936.

FREEDOM

1   My people and I have come to an agreement which satisfies us both. They are to say what they please, and I am to do what I please.

FREDERICK THE GREAT   (1712–86)   King of Prussia.

2   I have got no further than this: Every man has a right to utter what he thinks truth, and every other man has a right to knock him down for it. Martyrdom is the test.

SAMUEL JOHNSON   (1709–84)   British lexicographer.

3   It's often safer to be in chains than to be free.

FRANZ KAFKA   (1883–1924)   Czech novelist.

4   Freedom's just another word for nothing left to lose.

KRIS KRISTOFFERSON   (1936–   )   US film actor and folk musician.

5   Freedom is the right to tell people what they do not want to hear.

GEORGE ORWELL   (Eric Blair; 1903–50)   British novelist.

6   We have to believe in free will. We've got no choice.

ISAAC BASHEVIS SINGER   (1904–91)   Polish-born US writer.

7   It is by the goodness of God that in our country we have those three unspeakably precious things: freedom of speech, freedom of conscience, and the prudence never to practise either of them.

MARK TWAIN   (Samuel Langhorne Clemens; 1835–1910) US writer.

8   I disapprove of what you say, but I will defend to the
     death your right to say it.

VOLTAIRE (François-Marie Arouet; 1694–1778) French
writer.

FRIENDSHIP

1   Forsake not an old friend; for the new is not compar-
     able to him: a new friend is as new wine; when it is
     old, thou shalt drink it with pleasure.

BIBLE: ECCLESIASTICUS

2   Two may talk together under the same roof for
     many years, yet never really meet; and two others
     at first speech are old friends.

MARY CATHERWOOD (1847–1901) US writer.

3   There is nothing in the world I wouldn't do for
     Hope, and there is nothing he wouldn't do for me
     . . . We spend our lives doing nothing for each
     other.

BING CROSBY (Harry Lillis Crosby; 1904–77) US singer.
Referring to Bob Hope

4   Instead of loving your enemies, treat your friends a
     little better.

E. W. HOWE (1853–1937) US novelist.

5   Sir, I look upon every day to be lost, in which I do
     not make a new acquaintance.

SAMUEL JOHNSON (1709–84) British lexicographer.

6 Men seem to kick friendship around like a football, but it doesn't seem to crack. Women treat it as glass and it goes to pieces.

ANNE MORROW LINDBERGH (1906–) US poet.

7 Love is blind; friendship closes its eyes.

PROVERB

8 So long as we are loved by others I should say that we are almost indispensable; and no man is useless while he has a friend.

ROBERT LOUIS STEVENSON (1850–94) Scottish writer.

9 Such a good friend that she will throw all her acquaintances into the water for the pleasure of fishing them out again.

TALLEYRAND (Charles Maurice de Talleyrand-Périgord; 1754–1838) French politician.
Referring to Madame de Staël

10 We cherish our friends not for their ability to amuse us, but for ours to amuse them.

EVELYN WAUGH (1903–66) British novelist.

FUNERALS

1 This is the last time that I will take part as an amateur.

DANIEL-FRANÇOIS-ESPRIT AUBER (1782–1871) French composer.
Said at a funeral

2 'If you don't go to other men's funerals,' he told Father stiffly, 'they won't go to yours.'

CLARENCE SHEPARD DAY (1874–1935) US writer.

3   I bet you a hundred bucks he ain't in here.

CHARLES BANCROFT DILLINGHAM (1868–1934) US theatrical manager.
Referring to the escapologist Harry Houdini; said at his funeral, while carrying his coffin

4   When I die I want to decompose in a barrel of porter and have it served in all the pubs in Dublin.

J. P. DONLEAVY (1926–   ) US novelist.

5   It proves what they say, give the public what they want to see and they'll come out for it.

RED SKELTON (Richard Bernard Skelton; 1913–   ) US actor and comedian.
Said while attending the funeral in 1958 of Hollywood producer Harry Cohn. It has also been attributed to Samuel Goldwyn while attending Louis B. Mayer's funeral in 1957

FUTURE

1   Boast not thyself of tomorrow; for thou knowest not what a day may bring forth.

BIBLE: PROVERBS

2   *Future*, n That period of time in which our affairs prosper, our friends are true and our happiness is assured.

AMBROSE BIERCE (1842–?1914) US writer.

3   I never think of the future. It comes soon enough.

ALBERT EINSTEIN (1879–1955) German-born US physicist.

4 I have seen the future and it works.

LINCOLN STEFFENS (1866–1936) US journalist.
Speaking to Bernard Baruch after visiting the Soviet
Union, 1919

5 The future is made of the same stuff as the present.

SIMONE WEIL (1909–43) French philosopher.

GAMES

---

1 It is very wonderful to see persons of the best
sense passing away a dozen hours together in shuffling and dividing a pack of cards, with no other conversation but what is made up of a few game
phrases, and no other ideas but those of black or red
spots ranged together in different figures.

JOSEPH ADDISON (1672–1719) British essayist.

2 Life's too short for chess.

HENRY JAMES BYRON (1834–84) British dramatist and
actor.

3 I am still a victim of chess. It has all the beauty of
art – and much more. It cannot be commercialized.
Chess is much purer than art in its social position.

MARCEL DUCHAMP (1887–1968) French artist.

4 A man's idea in a card game is war – cool, devastat-
ing and pitiless. A lady's idea of it is a combination of
larceny, embezzlement and burglary.

FINLEY PETER DUNNE (1867–1936) US journalist.

5   I am sorry I have not learned to play at cards. It is very useful in life: it generates kindness and consolidates society.

SAMUEL JOHNSON (1709–84) British lexicographer.

GENERALIZATIONS

1   All generalizations are dangerous, even this one.

ALEXANDRE DUMAS, FILS (1824–95) French writer.

GIFTS

1   The manner of giving is worth more than the gift.

PIERRE CORNEILLE (1606–84) French dramatist.

GOLDWYNISMS

1   Too caustic? To hell with cost; we'll make the picture anyway.

2   We're overpaying him but he's worth it.

3   I am willing to admit that I may not always be right, but I am never wrong.

4   Anybody who goes to see a psychiatrist ought to have his head examined.

5   I'll give you a definite maybe.

6   A verbal contract isn't worth the paper it's written on.

7 We have all passed a lot of water since then.

8 Tell me, how did you love my picture?

GOOD

1 Evil comes at leisure like the disease; good comes in a hurry like the doctor.

G. K. CHESTERTON (1874–1936) British writer.

2 What is a weed? A plant whose virtues have not been discovered.

RALPH WALDO EMERSON (1803–82) US poet and essayist.

3 Do good by stealth, and blush to find it fame.

ALEXANDER POPE (1688–1744) British poet.

4 How far that little candle throws his beams!
So shines a good deed in a naughty world.

WILLIAM SHAKESPEARE (1564–1616) English dramatist.

5 Nothing can harm a good man, either in life or after death.

SOCRATES (469–399 BC) Athenian philosopher.

6 – My goodness those diamonds are lovely!
Goodness had nothing whatever to do with it.

MAE WEST (1892–1980) US actress.
Used in 1959 as the title of the first volume of her autobiography

GOSSIP

1   No one gossips about other people's secret virtues.

BERTRAND RUSSELL (1872–1970) British philosopher.

GOVERNMENT

1   One day the don't-knows will get in, and then where will we be?

SPIKE MILLIGAN (1918–) British comic actor and author.

2   Parliament is the longest running farce in the West End.

CYRIL SMITH (1928–) British Liberal politician.

HAPPINESS

1   Ask yourself whether you are happy, and you cease to be so.

JOHN STUART MILL (1806–73) British philosopher.

2   When a small child ... I thought that success spelled happiness. I was wrong. Happiness is like a butterfly which appears and delights us for one brief moment, but soon flits away.

ANNA PAVLOVA (1881–1931) Russian ballet dancer.

3   Happiness is an imaginary condition, formerly often attributed by the living to the dead, now usually attributed by adults to children, and by children to adults.

THOMAS SZASZ (1920–) US psychiatrist.

4   Happiness is no laughing matter.

RICHARD WHATELY (1787–1863) British churchman.

HASTE

1   In skating over thin ice, our safety is in our speed.

RALPH WALDO EMERSON (1803–82) US poet and
essayist.

HATE

1   I am free of all prejudice. I hate everyone equally.

W. C. FIELDS (1880–1946) US actor.

HOME

1   The house is well, but it is you, Your Majesty, who
have made me too great for my house.

FRANCIS BACON (1561–1626) English philosopher.
Reply when Elizabeth I remarked on the smallness of his
house

2   Home is the place where, when you have to go
there,
They have to take you in.

ROBERT FROST (1875–1963) US poet.

3   A man travels the world over in search of what he
needs and returns home to find it.

GEORGE MOORE (1852–1933) Irish writer and art critic.

HONOUR

1 Remember, men, we're fighting for this woman's honour; which is probably more than she ever did.

GROUCHO MARX (Julius Marx; 1895–1977) US comedian.

HOSPITALITY

1 Let brotherly love continue.
Be not forgetful to entertain strangers: for thereby some have entertained angels unawares.

BIBLE: HEBREWS

2 A constant guest is never welcome.

PROVERB

HOUSES OF PARLIAMENT

1 The House of Lords is like a glass of champagne that has stood for five days.

CLEMENT ATTLEE (1883–1967) British statesman and Labour prime minister.

2 A severe though not unfriendly critic of our institutions said that 'the cure for admiring the House of Lords was to go and look at it.'

WALTER BAGEHOT (1826–77) British economist and journalist.

3 The House of Lords is a model of how to care for the elderly.

FRANK FIELD (1942–   ) British politician.

4   The House of Lords must be the only institution in the world which is kept efficient by the persistent absenteeism of most of its members.

HERBERT SAMUEL (1870–1963) British Liberal statesman.

HUMAN NATURE

1   Upon the whole I dislike mankind: whatever people on the other side of the question may advance, they cannot deny that they are always surprised at hearing of a good action and never of a bad one.

JOHN KEATS (1795–1821) British poet.

2   No absolute is going to make the lion lie down with the lamb unless the lamb is inside.

D. H. LAWRENCE (1885–1930) British novelist.

HUMILITY

1   It is difficult to be humble. Even if you aim at humility, there is no guarantee that when you have attained the state you will not be proud of the feat.

BONAMY DOBRÉE (1891–1974) British scholar and writer.

2   The meek do not inherit the earth unless they are prepared to fight for their meekness.

H. J. LASKI (1893–1950) British political theorist.

3   I too had thoughts once of being an intellectual, but I found it too difficult.

ALBERT SCHWEITZER (1875–1965) French Protestant theologian, philosopher, and physician.

Remark made to an African who refused to perform a menial task on the grounds that he was an intellectual

HUMOUR

1 The marvellous thing about a joke with a double meaning is that it can only mean one thing.

RONNIE BARKER (1929–) British comedian.

2 Men will confess to treason, murder, arson, false teeth, or a wig. How many of them will own up to a lack of humour?

FRANK MORE COLBY (1865–1925) US editor.

3 It's hard to be funny when you have to be clean.

MAE WEST (1892–1980) US actress.

Some examples

4 I do most of my work sitting down; that's where I shine.

ROBERT BENCHLEY (1889–1945) US humorist.

5 Dear 338171 (May I call you 338?).

NOËL COWARD (1899–1973) British dramatist.
Starting a letter to T. E. Lawrence who had retired from public life to become Aircraftsman Brown, 338171

6 Please accept my resignation. I don't want to belong to any club that will accept me as a member.

GROUCHO MARX (Julius Marx; 1895–1977) US comedian.
Resigning from the Friar's Club in Hollywood

7   Oh, don't worry about Alan . . . Alan will always land on somebody's feet.

DOROTHY PARKER (1893–1967) US writer.
Said of her husband on the day their divorce became final

HUNTING

1   There is a passion for *hunting something* deeply implanted in the human breast.

CHARLES DICKENS (1812–70) British novelist.

2   It is very strange, and very melancholy, that the paucity of human pleasures should persuade us ever to call hunting one of them.

SAMUEL JOHNSON (1709–84) British lexicographer.

3   When a man wantonly destroys one of the works of man we call him a vandal. When he destroys one of the works of God we call him a sportsman.

JOSEPH WOOD KRUTCH (1893–1970) US essayist.

4   When a man wants to murder a tiger he calls it sport; when a tiger wants to murder him he calls it ferocity.

GEORGE BERNARD SHAW (1856–1950) Irish dramatist and critic.

5   The birds seem to consider the muzzle of my gun as their safest position.

SYDNEY SMITH (1771–1845) English writer and clergyman.

6   It is the sport of kings, the image of war without its guilt, and only five-and-twenty per cent of its danger.

R. S. SURTEES (1803–64) English novelist.

7   The English country gentleman galloping after a fox – the unspeakable in full pursuit of the uneatable.

OSCAR WILDE (1854–1900) Irish-born British dramatist.

HYPOCRISY

1   Man is the only animal that can remain on friendly terms with the victims he intends to eat until he eats them.

SAMUEL BUTLER (1835–1902) British writer.

2   The book written against fame and learning has the author's name on the title-page.

RALPH WALDO EMERSON (1803–82) US poet and essayist.

IDEALISM

1   If a man hasn't discovered something that he would die for, he isn't fit to live.

MARTIN LUTHER KING (1929–68) US Black civil-rights leader.

2   An idealist is one who, on noticing that a rose smells better than a cabbage, concludes that it will also make better soup.

H. L. MENCKEN (1880–1956) US journalist.

3   A radical is a man with both feet firmly planted in the air.

FRANKLIN D. ROOSEVELT (1882–1945) US Democratic president.

IDEAS

1   What was once thought can never be unthought.

FRIEDRICH DÜRRENMATT (1921–) Swiss writer.

2   A stand can be made against invasion by an army; no stand can be made against invasion by an idea.

VICTOR HUGO (1802–85) French writer.

IDLENESS

1   Idleness is only the refuge of weak minds.

EARL OF CHESTERFIELD (1694–1773) English statesman.

2   I like work; it fascinates me. I can sit and look at it for hours. I love to keep it by me; the idea of getting rid of it nearly breaks my heart.

JEROME K. JEROME (1859–1927) British humorist.

IGNORANCE

1   I wish you would read a little poetry sometimes. Your ignorance cramps my conversation.

ANTHONY HOPE (Sir Anthony Hope Hawkins; 1863–1933) British novelist.

2   What you don't know would make a great book.

SYDNEY SMITH (1771–1845) British clergyman and
essayist.

3   Ignorance is like a delicate exotic fruit; touch it, and
the bloom is gone.

OSCAR WILDE (1854–1900) Irish-born British dramatist.

IMPERFECTION

1   When you have faults, do not fear to abandon them.

CONFUCIUS (K'ung Fu-tzu; 551–479 BC) Chinese
philosopher.

2   We only confess our little faults to persuade people
that we have no large ones.

DUC DE LA ROCHEFOUCAULD (1613–80) French writer.

3   We are none of us infallible – not even the youngest
of us.

WILLIAM HEPWORTH THOMPSON (1810–86) British
academic.
Referring to G. W. Balfour, who was a junior fellow of
Trinity College at the time

INATTENTION

1   That should assure us of at least forty-five minutes
of undisturbed privacy.

DOROTHY PARKER (1893–1967) US writer.
Pressing a button marked NURSE during a stay in
hospital

2   I murdered my grandmother this morning.

FRANKLIN D. ROOSEVELT (1882–1945) US Democratic president.
His habitual greeting to any guest at the White House he suspected of paying no attention to what he said

INDECISION

1   I must have a prodigious quantity of mind; it takes me as much as a week, sometimes, to make it up.

MARK TWAIN (Samuel Langhorne Clemens; 1835–1910) US writer.

INDISPENSABILITY

1   She was one of those indispensables of whom one makes the discovery, when they are gone, that one can get on quite as well without them.

ALDOUS HUXLEY (1894–1964) British novelist.

INFERIORITY

1   No one can make you feel inferior without your consent.

ELEÁNOR ROOSEVELT (1884–1962) US writer and lecturer.

INGRATITUDE

1   Our gratitude to most benefactors is the same as
    our feeling for dentists who have pulled our teeth.
    We acknowledge the good they have done and the
    evil from which they have delivered us, but we re-
    member the pain they occasioned and do not love
    them very much.

    NICOLAS CHAMFORT (1741–94) French writer.

INJUSTICE

1   When one has been threatened with a great injus-
    tice, one accepts a smaller as a favour.

    JANE WELSH CARLYLE (1801–66) The wife of Thomas
    Carlyle.

2   I feel as a horse must feel when the beautiful cup is
    given to the jockey.

    EDGAR DEGAS (1834–1917) French artist.
    On seeing one of his pictures sold at auction

INSENSITIVITY

1   One would have to have a heart of stone to read the
    death of Little Nell without laughing.

    OSCAR WILDE (1854–1900) Irish-born British dramatist.
    Lecturing upon Dickens

INSINCERITY

1   Experience teaches you that the man who looks you straight in the eye, particularly if he adds a firm handshake, is hiding something.

CLIFTON FADIMAN (1904–) US writer.

INSULTS

1   Like a cushion, he always bore the impress of the last man who sat on him.

DAVID LLOYD GEORGE (1863–1945) British Liberal statesman.
Referring to Lord Derby

2   When they circumcised Herbert Samuel they threw away the wrong bit.

DAVID LLOYD GEORGE

3   She looked as though butter wouldn't melt in her mouth —or anywhere else.

ELSA LANCHESTER (1902–86) British-born US actress.
Referring to Maureen O'Hara

4   A triumph of the embalmer's art.

GORE VIDAL (1925–) US novelist.
Referring to Ronald Reagan

5   A typical triumph of modern science to find the only part of Randolph that was not malignant and remove it.

EVELYN WAUGH (1903–66) British novelist.
Remarking upon the news that Randolph Churchill had had a noncancerous lung removed

6   You have Van Gogh's ear for music.

BILLY WILDER (Samuel Wilder; 1906–) Austrian-born
US film director.
Said to Cliff Osmond

7   I have always said about Tony that he immatures
with age.

HAROLD WILSON (1916–) British politician and prime
minister.
Referring to Anthony Wedgwood Benn

INTELLECT

1   An intellectual is a man who doesn't know how to
park a bike.

SPIRO AGNEW (1918–) US politician.

2   Intellectuals are people who believe that ideas are of
more importance than values. That is to say, their
own ideas and other people's values.

GERALD BRENAN (Edward Fitzgerald Brenan; 1894–
1987) British writer.

3   The highest intellects, like the tops of mountains,
are the first to catch and to reflect the dawn.

LORD MACAULAY (1800–59) British historian.

4   The higher the voice the smaller the intellect.

ERNEST NEWMAN (1868–1959) British music critic.

5   What is a highbrow? It is a man who has found
something more interesting than women.

EDGAR WALLACE (1875–1932) British thriller writer.

6   All the unhappy marriages come from the husbands
     having brains. What good are brains to a man? They
     only unsettle him.

     P. G. WODEHOUSE (1881–1975) British humorous
     novelist.

IRELAND

1   All races have produced notable economists, with
     the exception of the Irish who doubtless can protest
     their devotion to higher arts.

     JOHN KENNETH GALBRAITH (1908–   ) US economist.

2   Worth seeing? yes; but not worth going to see.

     SAMUEL JOHNSON (1709–84) British lexicographer.
     Referring to the Giant's Causeway

3   The Irish are a fair people; – they never speak well
     of one another.

     SAMUEL JOHNSON

4   The problem with Ireland is that it's a country full of
     genius, but with absolutely no talent.

     HUGH LEONARD (1926–   ) Irish dramatist.
     Said during an interview

5   It is a city where you can see a sparrow fall to the
     ground, and God watching it.

     CONOR CRUISE O'BRIEN (1917–   ) Irish diplomat and
     writer.
     Referring to Dublin

6   The English should give Ireland home rule – and re-
     serve the motion picture rights.

W<small>ILL</small> R<small>OGERS</small> (1879–1935) US actor and humorist.

JEALOUSY

1   The others were only my wives. But you, my dear, will be my widow.

S<small>ACHA</small> G<small>UITRY</small> (1885–1957) French actor and dramatist. Allaying his fifth wife's jealousy of his previous wives

JEWS

1   The gentleman will please remember that when his half-civilized ancestors were hunting the wild boar in Silesia, mine were princes of the earth.

J<small>UDAH</small> P<small>HILIP</small> B<small>ENJAMIN</small> (1811–84) US politician. Replying to a senator of Germanic origin who had made an antisemitic remark

2   I believe that the Jews have made a contribution to the human condition out of all proportion to their numbers: I believe them to be an immense people. Not only have they supplied the world with two leaders of the stature of Jesus Christ and Karl Marx, but they have even indulged in the luxury of following neither one nor the other.

P<small>ETER</small> U<small>STINOV</small> (1921–   ) British actor.

JUDGMENT

1   Consider what you think justice requires, and decide accordingly. But never give your reasons; for your judgement will probably be right, but your reasons will certainly be wrong.

LORD MANSFIELD (1705–93) British judge and politician.
Advice given to a new colonial governor

2   Everyone complains of his memory, but no one complains of his judgement.

DUC DE LA ROCHEFOUCAULD (1613–80) French writer.

JUSTICE

1   I'm arm'd with more than complete steel –
The justice of my quarrel.

CHRISTOPHER MARLOWE (1564–93) English dramatist.

2   In England, Justice is open to all, like the Ritz hotel.

JAMES MATHEW (1830–1908) British judge.
Also attrib. to Lord Darling

KINDNESS

1   I love thee for a heart that's kind –
Not for the knowledge in thy mind.

W. H. DAVIES (1871–1940) British poet.

2   So many gods, so many creeds,
So many paths that wind and wind,
While just the art of being kind
Is all the sad world needs.

ELLA WHEELER WILCOX (1850–1919) US poet.

KNOWLEDGE

1   The fox knows many things – the hedgehog one *big* one.

ARCHILOCHUS (c. 680–c. 640 BC) Greek poet.

2 It is the province of knowledge to speak and it is the privilege of wisdom to listen.

OLIVER WENDELL HOLMES (1809–94) US writer.

3 All knowledge is of itself of some value. There is nothing so minute or inconsiderable, that I would not rather know it than not.

SAMUEL JOHNSON (1709–84) British lexicographer.

4 Knowledge is of two kinds. We know a subject ourselves, or we know where we can find information upon it.

SAMUEL JOHNSON

5 Learning is a treasure which accompanies its owner everywhere.

PROVERB

LEADERSHIP

1 'She still seems to me in her own way a person born to command,' said Luce . . .
'I wonder if anyone is born to obey,' said Isabel.
'That may be why people command rather badly, that
they have no suitable material to work on.'

IVY COMPTON-BURNETT (1892–1969) British novelist.

2 Let me pass, I have to follow them, I am their leader.

ALEXANDRE AUGUSTE LEDRU-ROLLIN (1807–74) French lawyer and politician.

Trying to force his way through a mob during the Revolution of 1848, of which he was one of the chief instigators. A similar remark is attributed to Bonar Law.

LEAVING

1 I will undoubtedly have to seek what is happily known as gainful employment, which I am glad to say does not describe holding public office.

DEAN ACHESON (1893–1971) US lawyer and statesman.

2 It is amazing how nice people are to you when they know you are going away.

MICHAEL ARLEN (1895–1956) British novelist.

3 It is never any good dwelling on goodbyes. It is not the being together that it prolongs, it is the parting.

ELIZABETH BIBESCO (1897–1945) British writer.

4 Absence is to love what wind is to fire; it extinguishes the small, it inflames the great.

BUSSY-RABUTIN (Roger de Rabutin, Comte de Bussy; 1618–93) French soldier and writer.

5 All farewells should be sudden.

LORD BYRON (1788–1824) British poet.

6 Retirement from the concert world is like giving up smoking. You have got to finish completely.

BENIAMINO GIGLI (1890–1957) Italian tenor.

7 He had said he had known many kicked down stairs, but he never knew any kicked up stairs before.

LORD HALIFAX (1633–95) English statesman.

8   Have you ever been out for a late autumn walk in the closing part of the afternoon, and suddenly looked up to realize that the leaves have practically all gone? And the sun has set and the day gone before you knew it – and with that a cold wind blows across the landscape? That's retirement.

STEPHEN LEACOCK (1869–1944) English-born Canadian economist and humorist.

9   There comes a time in every man's life when he must make way for an older man.

REGINALD MAUDLING (1917–77) British politician. Remark made on being replaced in the shadow cabinet by John Davies, his elder by four years

10   Eating's going to be a whole new ball game. I may even have to buy a new pair of trousers.

LESTER PIGGOT (1935–) British champion jockey. On his retirement

11   Fear no more the heat o' the sun,
Nor the furious winter's rages;
Thou thy worldly task hast done,
Home art gone and ta'en thy wages.

WILLIAM SHAKESPEARE (1564–1616) English dramatist.

12   Good night, good night! Parting is such sweet sorrow
That I shall say good night till it be morrow.

WILLIAM SHAKESPEARE

13   When a man retires and time is no longer a matter of urgent importance, his colleagues generally present him with a clock.

R. C. SHERRIFF (1896–1975) British author.

LIFE

1   Life is rather like a tin of sardines – we're all of us looking for the key.

    ALAN BENNETT (1934–   ) British playwright.

2   Life is a tragedy when seen in close-up, but a comedy in long-shot.

    CHARLIE CHAPLIN (Sir Charles Spencer C.; 1889–1977) British film actor.

3   Life is a maze in which we take the wrong turning before we have learnt to walk.

    CYRIL CONNOLLY (1903–74) British journalist.

4   Life is like a sewer. What you get out of it depends on what you put into it.

    TOM LEHRER (1928–   ) US university teacher and songwriter.

LONDON

1   I think the full tide of human existence is at Charing-Cross.

    SAMUEL JOHNSON (1709–84) British lexicographer.

2   When a man is tired of London, he is tired of life; for there is in London all that life can afford.

    SAMUEL JOHNSON

3   Crossing Piccadilly Circus.

    JOSEPH THOMSON (1858–95) Scottish explorer.
    His reply when asked by J. M. Barrie what was the most hazardous part of his expedition to Africa

LOVE

1   Love is, above all, the gift of oneself.

JEAN ANOUILH (1910–87) French dramatist.

2   Many a man has fallen in love with a girl in a light so dim he would not have chosen a suit by it.

MAURICE CHEVALIER (1888–1972) French singer and actor.

3   We don't believe in rheumatism and true love until after the first attack.

MARIE EBNER VON ESCHENBACH (1830–1916) Austrian writer.

4   Love's like the measles – all the worse when it comes late in life.

DOUGLAS WILLIAM JERROLD (1803–57) British dramatist.

5   Love does not consist in gazing at each other but in looking together in the same direction.

ANTOINE DE SAINT-EXUPÉRY (1900–44) French novelist and aviator.

6   True love's the gift which God has given
    To man alone beneath the heaven.

WALTER SCOTT (1771–1832) Scottish novelist.

MANNERS

1   On the Continent people have good food; in England people have good table manners.

GEORGE MIKES (1912–87) Hungarian-born British writer.

2   Good breeding consists in concealing how much we think of ourselves and how little we think of other persons.

    MARK TWAIN (Samuel Langhorne Clemens; 1835–1910) US writer.

MARRIAGE

1   *Marriage*, n. The state or condition of a community consisting of a master, a mistress and two slaves, making in all two.

    AMBROSE BIERCE (1842–?1914) US writer and journalist.

2   Marriage has many pains, but celibacy has no pleasures.

    SAMUEL JOHNSON (1709–84) British lexicographer.

3   One doesn't have to get anywhere in a marriage. It's not a public conveyance.

    IRIS MURDOCH (1919–) Irish-born British novelist.

4   A loving wife will do anything for her husband except stop criticising and trying to improve him.

    J. B. PRIESTLEY (1894–1984) British novelist.

5   A married couple are well suited when both partners usually feel the need for a quarrel at the same time.

    JEAN ROSTAND (1894–1977) French biologist and writer.

6   Never feel remorse for what you have thought about your wife; she has thought much worse things about you.

    JEAN ROSTAND

7   It takes two to make a marriage a success and only
    one a failure.

    HERBERT SAMUEL (1870–1963) British Liberal statesman.

8   My definition of marriage: . . . .it resembles a pair of
    shears, so joined that they cannot be separated; of-
    ten moving in opposite directions, yet always pun-
    ishing anyone who comes between them.

    SYDNEY SMITH (1771–1845) British clergyman and
    essayist.

9   A man should not insult his wife publicly, at parties.
    He should insult her in the privacy of the home.

    JAMES THURBER (1894–1961) US humorist.

10 Twenty years of romance makes a woman look like
    a ruin; but twenty years of marriage make her
    something like a public building.

    OSCAR WILDE (1854–1900) Irish-born British dramatist.

11 The best part of married life is the fights. The rest
    is merely so-so.

    THORNTON WILDER (1897–1975) US novelist and
    dramatist.

MEDICINE

1   I am dying with the help of too many physicians.

    ALEXANDER THE GREAT (356–323 BC) King of
    Macedon.

2   One of the most difficult things to contend with in a hospital is the assumption on the part of the staff that because you have lost your gall bladder you have also lost your mind.

JEAN KERR (1923–   ) US dramatist.

MEN

1   I base everything on the idea that all men are basically just seven years old.

JOAN COLLINS (1933–   ) British actress.

2   The male ego with few exceptions is elephantine to start with.

BETTE DAVIS (Ruth Elizabeth D.; 1908–89) US actress.

3   I never hated a man enough to give him diamonds back.

ZSA ZSA GABOR (1919–   ) Hungarian-born US film star.

4   Sometimes I think if there was a third sex men wouldn't get so much as a glance from me.

AMANDA VAIL (Warren Miller; 1921–66) US writer.

5   A man in the house is worth two in the street.

MAE WEST (1892–1980) US actress.

MEN AND WOMEN

1   The reason that husbands and wives do not understand each other is because they belong to different sexes.

DOROTHY DIX (Elizabeth Meriwether Gilmer; 1861–1951) US journalist and writer.

2 Where young boys plan for what they will achieve and attain, young girls plan for whom they will achieve and attain.

CHARLOTTE PERKINS GILMAN (1860–1935) US writer.

3 Fighting is essentially a masculine idea; a woman's weapon is her tongue.

HERMIONE GINGOLD (1897–1987) British actress.

4 Strange difference of sex, that time and circumstance, which enlarge the views of most men, narrows the views of women almost invariably.

THOMAS HARDY (1840–1928) British novelist.

5 Man has his will, – but woman has her way.

OLIVER WENDELL HOLMES (1809–94) US writer.

6 A woman needs a man like a fish needs a bicycle.

PROVERB

7 I do, and I also wash and iron them.

DENIS THATCHER (1915–) British businessman, husband of Margaret Thatcher.
Replying to the question "Who wears the pants in this house?"

8 When a man confronts catastrophe on the road, he looks in his purse – but a woman looks in her mirror.

MARGARET TURNBULL (fl. 1920s–1942) US writer.

9   Why are women . . . so much more interesting to men than men are to women?

VIRGINIA WOOLF (1882–1941) British novelist.

MISFORTUNE

1   Calamities are of two kinds. Misfortune to ourselves and good fortune to others.

AMBROSE BIERCE (1842–?1914) US writer and journalist.

2   We are all strong enough to bear the misfortunes of others.

DUC DE LA ROCHEFOUCAULD (1613–80) French writer.

MISTAKES

1   Better send them a Papal Bull.

LORD CURZON (1859–1925) British politician.
Written in the margin of a Foreign Office document. The phrase 'the monks of Mount Athos were violating their vows' had been misprinted as ' . . . violating their cows'.

2   Yes, once – many, many years ago. I thought I had made a wrong decision. Of course, it turned out that I had been right all along. But I was wrong to have *thought* that I was wrong.

JOHN FOSTER DULLES (1888–1959) US politician.
On being asked whether he had ever been wrong

3   The man who makes no mistakes does not usually make anything.

EDWARD JOHN PHELPS (1822–1900) US lawyer and diplomat.

4   The follies which a man regrets the most in his life, are those which he didn't commit when he had the opportunity.

HELEN ROWLAND (1876–1950) US writer.

5   What time is the next swan?

LEO SLEZAK (1873–1946) Czechoslovakian-born tenor. When the mechanical swan left the stage without him during a performance of *Lohengrin*

MISTRUST

1   The lion and the calf shall lie down together but the calf won't get much sleep.

WOODY ALLEN (Allen Stewart Konigsberg; 1935–   ) US film actor.

MONEY

1   A man who has a million dollars is as well off as if he were rich.

JOHN JACOB ASTOR (1763–1848) US millionaire.

2   Money is like muck, not good except it be spread.

FRANCIS BACON (1561–1626) English philosopher.
See also MURCHISON

3   Money, it turned out, was exactly like sex, you thought of nothing else if you didn't have it and thought of other things if you did.

JAMES BALDWIN (1924–87) US writer.

4   If you can actually count your money you are not really a rich man.

J. PAUL GETTY (1892–1976) US oil magnate.

5   There are few ways in which a man can be more innocently employed than in getting money.

SAMUEL JOHNSON (1709–84) British lexicographer.

6   You don't seem to realize that a poor person who is unhappy is in a better position than a rich person who is unhappy. Because the poor person has hope. He thinks money would help.

JEAN KERR (1923–   ) US dramatist.

7   What's a thousand dollars? Mere chicken feed. A poultry matter.

GROUCHO MARX (Julius Marx; 1895–1977) US comedian.

8   Money can't buy friends, but you can get a better class of enemy.

SPIKE MILLIGAN (1918–   ) British comic actor and author.

9   Money is like manure. If you spread it around it does a lot of good. But if you pile it up in one place it stinks like hell.

CLINT MURCHISON JNR (1895–1969) US industrialist. Following BACON

10   God shows his contempt for wealth by the kind of person he selects to receive it.

AUSTIN O'MALLEY (1858–1932) US writer.

11   The trouble, Mr Goldwyn is that you are only inter-
     ested in art and I am only interested in money.

     GEORGE BERNARD SHAW (1856–1950) Irish dramatist
     and critic.
     Turning down Goldwyn's offer to buy the screen rights
     of his plays

12   It is the wretchedness of being rich that you have to
     live with rich people.

     LOGAN PEARSALL SMITH (1865–1946) US writer.

13   That's right. 'Taint yours, and 'taint mine.

     MARK TWAIN (Samuel Langhorne Clemens; 1835–1910)
     US writer.
     Agreeing with a friend's comment that the money of a
     particular rich industrialist was 'tainted'.

14   There's something about a crowd like that that
     brings a lump to my wallet.

     ELI WALLACH (1915–   ) US actor.
     Remarking upon the long line of people at the box office
     before one of his performances

15   You can be young without money but you can't be
     old without it.

     TENNESSEE WILLIAMS (1911–83) US dramatist.

MORALITY

1   Give me chastity and continence, but not yet.

     ST AUGUSTINE OF HIPPO (354–430) Bishop of Hippo.

2   No morality can be founded on authority, even if the
     authority were divine.

A. J. AYER (1910–89) British philosopher.

3 What is moral is what you feel good after, and what is immoral is what you feel bad after.

ERNEST HEMINGWAY (1899–1961) US novelist.

4 The Puritan hated bear-baiting, not because it gave pain to the bear, but because it gave pleasure to the spectators.

LORD MACAULAY (1800–59) British historian.

5 Puritanism – The haunting fear that someone, somewhere, may be happy.

H. L. MENCKEN (1880–1956) US journalist.

6 Morality consists in suspecting other people of not being legally married.

GEORGE BERNARD SHAW (1856–1950) Irish dramatist and critic.

7 The so-called new morality is too often the old immorality condoned.

LORD SHAWCROSS (1902–) British Labour politician and lawyer.

8 Moral indignation is in most cases 2 percent moral, 48 percent indignation and 50 percent envy.

VITTORIO DE SICA (1901–74) Italian film director.

MORTALITY

1 They are not long, the days of wine and roses.

ERNEST DOWSON (1867–1900) British lyric poet.

2   All humane things are subject to decay,
And, when Fate summons, Monarchs must obey.

JOHN DRYDEN (1631–1700) British poet and dramatist.

3   A little rule, a little sway,
A sunbeam in a winter's day,
Is all the proud and mighty have
Between the cradle and the grave.

JOHN DYER (1700–58) British poet.

4   Is life a boon?
If so, it must befall
That Death, whene'er he call,
Must call too soon.

W. S. GILBERT (1836–1911) British dramatist.
The lines are written on Arthur Sullivan's memorial in
the Embankment gardens

5   The boast of heraldry, the pomp of pow'r,
And all that beauty, all that wealth e'er gave,
Awaits alike th' inevitable hour,
The paths of glory lead but to the grave.

THOMAS GRAY (1716–71) British poet.

6   I expect to pass through this world but once; any
good thing therefore that I can do, or any kindness
that I can show to any fellow-creature, let me do it
now; let me not defer or neglect it, for I shall not
pass this way again.

STEPHEN GRELLET (1773–1855) French-born US
missionary.
Attrib.

7   I am moved to pity, when I think of the brevity of human life, seeing that of all this host of men not one will still be alive in a hundred years' time.

XERXES (d. 465 BC) King of Persia.
On surveying his army

MUSIC

1   The music teacher came twice each week to bridge the awful gap between Dorothy and Chopin.

GEORGE ADE (1866–1944) US dramatist and humorist.

2   Brass bands are all very well in their place – outdoors and several miles away.

THOMAS BEECHAM (1879–1961) British conductor.

3   The English may not like music – but they absolutely love the noise it makes.

THOMAS BEECHAM

4   The sound of the harpsichord resembles that of a bird-cage played with toasting-forks.

THOMAS BEECHAM

5   People are wrong when they say the opera isn't what it used to be. It is what it used to be. That's what's wrong with it.

NOËL COWARD (1899–1973) British dramatist.

6   Composing a piece of music is very feminine. It is sensitive, emotional, contemplative. By comparison, doing housework is positively masculine.

BARBARA KOLB (1939–   ) US composer.

7   To be played with both hands in the pocket.

ERIK SATIE (1866–1925) French composer.
Direction on one of his piano pieces

8   After I die, I shall return to earth as a gatekeeper of
a bordello and I won't let any of you – not a one of
you – enter!

ARTURO TOSCANINI (1867–1957) Italian conductor.
Rebuking an incompetent orchestra

NAKEDNESS

1   JOURNALIST. Didn't you have anything on?
M. M. I had the radio on.

MARILYN MONROE (Norma-Jean Baker; 1926–62) US
film star.

NONCOMMITMENT

1   We know what happens to people who stay in the
middle of the road. They get run over.

ANEURIN BEVAN (1897–1960) British Labour politician.

2   The Right Hon. gentleman has sat so long on the
fence that the iron has entered his soul.

DAVID LLOYD GEORGE (1863–1945) British Liberal
statesman.
Referring to Sir John Simon

OBESITY

1   Outside every fat man there is an even fatter man trying to close in.

KINGSLEY AMIS (1922–) British novelist.
See also ORWELL

2   I'm fat, but I'm thin inside. Has it ever struck you that there's a thin man inside every fat man, just as they say there's a statue inside every block of stone?

GEORGE ORWELL (Eric Blair; 1903–50) British novelist.
See also AMIS

3   My advice if you insist on slimming: Eat as much as you like – just don't swallow it.

HARRY SECOMBE (1921–) Welsh singer, actor, and comedian.

OBITUARIES

1   With the newspaper strike on I wouldn't consider it.

BETTE DAVIS (Ruth Elizabeth Davis; 1908–89) US film star.
When told that a rumour was spreading that she had died

2   I've just read that I am dead. Don't forget to delete me from your list of subscribers.

RUDYARD KIPLING (1865–1936) Indian-born British writer.
Writing to a magazine that had mistakenly published an announcement of his death

3   Reports of my death are greatly exaggerated.

MARK TWAIN (Samuel Langhorne Clemens; 1835–1910)
US writer.
On learning that his obituary had been published

OCCUPATIONS

Actors

1 For an actress to be a success she must have the face of Venus, the brains of Minerva, the grace of Terpsichore, the memory of Macaulay, the figure of Juno, and the hide of a rhinoceros.

ETHEL BARRYMORE (1897–1959) US actress.

2 An actor is something less than a man, while an actress is something more than a woman.

RICHARD BURTON (1925–84) British actor.

3 When an actor has money he doesn't send letters, he sends telegrams.

ANTON CHEKHOV (1860–1904) Russian dramatist.

4 Show me a great actor and I'll show you a lousy husband. Show me a great actress, and you've seen the devil.

W. C. FIELDS (1880–1946) US actor.

5 Have patience with the jealousies and petulance of actors, for their hour is their eternity.

RICHARD GARNETT (1835–1906) British writer.

6 Actresses will happen in the best regulated families.

OLIVER HERFORD (1863–1935) British-born US humorist.

7 Some of the greatest love affairs I've known involved one actor – unassisted.

WILSON MIZNER (1876–1933) US writer and wit.

8 A character actor is one who cannot act and therefore makes an elaborate study of disguise and stage tricks by which acting can be grotesquely simulated.

GEORGE BERNARD SHAW (1856–1950) Irish dramatist and critic.

9 An actor is never so great as when he reminds you of an animal – falling like a cat, lying like a dog, moving like a fox.

FRANÇOIS TRUFFAUT (1932–84) French film director.

10 Every actor in his heart believes everything bad that's printed about him.

ORSON WELLES (1915–85) US film director.

11 You can pick out actors by the glazed look that comes into their eyes when the conversation wanders away from themselves.

MICHAEL WILDING (1912–79) British actor.

Artists

12 Modern art is what happens when painters stop looking at girls and persuade themselves that they have a better idea.

JOHN CIARDI (1916–) US poet and critic.

13 There has never been a boy painter, nor can there be. The art requires a long apprenticeship, being *mechanical* as well as intellectual.

JOHN CONSTABLE (1776–1837) British landscape painter.

14 It is very good advice to believe only what an artist does, rather than what he says about his work.

DAVID HOCKNEY (1937–) British painter.

15 There is nothing more difficult for a truly creative painter than to paint a rose, because before he can do so he has first to forget all the roses that were ever painted.

HENRI MATISSE (1869–1954) French painter and sculptor.

16 Artists, as a rule, do not live in the purple; they live mainly in the red.

LORD PEARCE (1901–85) British judge.

17 There are painters who transform the sun into a yellow spot, but there are others who, thanks to their art and intelligence, transform a yellow spot into the sun.

PABLO PICASSO (1881–1973) Spanish painter.

18 An artist must know how to convince others of the truth of his lies.

PABLO PICASSO

19 The artist who always paints the same scene pleases the public for the sole reason that it recognises him with ease and thinks itself a connoisseur.

ALFRED STEVENS (1818–75) British artist.

Authors

20 When I want to read a novel I write one.

BENJAMIN DISRAELI (1804–81) British statesman.

21 The author who speaks about his own books is almost as bad as a mother who talks about her own children.

BENJAMIN DISRAELI

22 The best way to become a successful writer is to read good writing, remember it, and then forget where you remember it from.

GENE FOWLER (1890–1960) US author.

23 No author is a man of genius to his publisher.

HEINRICH HEINE (1797–1856) German poet and writer.

24 Abuse is often of service. There is nothing so dangerous to an author as silence.

SAMUEL JOHNSON (1709–84) British lexicographer.

25 No man but a blockhead ever wrote except for money.

SAMUEL JOHNSON

26 Most writers regard truth as their most valuable possession, and therefore are most economical in its use.

MARK TWAIN (Samuel Langhorne Clemens; 1835–1910) US writer.

Booksellers

27 Gentlemen, you must not mistake me. I admit that he is the sworn foe of our nation, and, if you will, of the whole human race. But, gentlemen, we must be just to our enemy. We must not forget that he once shot a bookseller.

THOMAS CAMPBELL (1777–1844) British poet.
Excusing himself in proposing a toast to Napoleon at a literary dinner

Clergy

28 It is no accident that the symbol of a bishop is a crook, and the sign of an archbishop is a double-cross.

DOM GREGORY DIX (1901–52) British monk.

29 How can a bishop marry? How can he flirt? The most he can say is, 'I will see you in the vestry after service.'

SYDNEY SMITH (1771–1845) British clergyman and essayist.

Cooks

30 We may live without friends; we may live without books;
But civilized man cannot live without cooks.

OWEN MEREDITH (Robert Bulmer-Lytton, 1st Earl of Lytton; 1831–91) British statesman and poet.

31 The only good thing about him is his cook. The world visits his dinners, not him.

MOLIÈRE (Jean Baptiste Poquelin; 1622–73) French dramatist.

32 The cook was a good cook, as cooks go; and as cooks go, she went.

SAKI (Hector Hugh Munro; 1870–1916) British writer.

Critics

33 Critics! . . . Those cut-throat bandits in the paths of fame.

ROBERT BURNS (1759–96) Scottish poet.

34 I always get the heaves in the presence of critics.

GENE FOWLER (1890–1960) US author.

35 Asking a working writer what he thinks about critics is like asking a lamp-post how it feels about dogs.

CHRISTOPHER HAMPTON (1946–) British writer and dramatist.

36 A drama critic is a person who surprises the playwright by informing him what he meant.

WILSON MIZNER (1876–1933) US writer and wit.

37 A critic is a legless man who teaches running.

CHANNING POLLOCK

38 A critic is a man who knows the way but can't drive the car.

KENNETH TYNAN (1927–80) British theatre critic.

39 Has anybody ever seen a dramatic critic in the daytime? Of course not. They come out after dark, up to no good.

P. G. WODEHOUSE (1881–1975) British humorous novelist.

Doctors

40 The threat of a neglected cold is for doctors what the threat of purgatory is for priests – a gold mine.

SÉBASTIEN CHAMFORT

41 God heals and the doctor takes the fee.

BENJAMIN FRANKLIN (1706–90) US scientist and statesman.

42 The doctor found, when she was dead, Her last disorder mortal.

OLIVER GOLDSMITH Irish-born British writer.

43 Doctors think a lot of patients are cured who have simply quit in disgust.

DON HEROLD

44 What I call a good patient is one who, having found a good physician, sticks to him till he dies.

OLIVER WENDELL HOLMES (1809–94) US writer.

45 Doctors will have more lives to answer for in the next world than even we generals.

NAPOLEON I (Napoleon Bonaparte; 1769–1821) French Emperor.

46 A young doctor makes a humpy graveyard.

PROVERB

47 There are worse occupations in this world than feeling a woman's pulse.

LAURENCE STERNE (1713–68) Irish-born British writer.

48 He has been a doctor a year now and has had two patients, no, three, I think – yes, it was three; I attended their funerals.

MARK TWAIN (Samuel Langhorne Clemens; 1835–1910) US writer.

49 Doctors are men who prescribe medicines of which they know little, to cure diseases of which they know less, in human beings of whom they know nothing.

VOLTAIRE (François-Marie Arouet; 1694–1778) French writer.

Editors

50 Where were you fellows when the paper was blank?

FRED ALLEN (1894–1956) US comedian.
Said to writers who heavily edited one of his scripts

51 An editor should have a pimp for a brother, so he'd have somebody to look up to.

GENE FOWLER (1890–1960) US author.

52 There are just two people entitled to refer to themselves as "we"; one is a newspaper editor and the other is a fellow with a tapeworm.

BILL NYE

53 An editor is one who separates the wheat from the chaff and prints the chaff.

ADLAI STEVENSON (1900–65) US statesman.

Farmers

54 Our Farmers round, well pleased with constant gain,
Like other farmers, flourish and complain.

GEORGE CRABBE (1754–1832) British poet.

55 A good farmer is nothing more nor less than a handy man with a sense of humus.

E. B. WHITE (1899–1985) US journalist and humorist.

Journalists

56 Doctors bury their mistakes. Lawyers hang them. But journalists put theirs on the front page.

ANONYMOUS

57 'Christianity, of course but why journalism?'

ARTHUR BALFOUR (1848–1930) British statesman.
In reply to Frank Harris's remark, '. . . all the faults of
the age come from Christianity and journalism'

58 It was long ago in my life as a simple reporter that I decided that facts must never get in the way of truth.

JAMES CAMERON (1911–85) British journalist.

59 Journalism largely consists of saying 'Lord Jones is dead' to people who never knew Lord Jones was alive.

G. K. CHESTERTON (1874–1936) British writer.

60 Literature is the art of writing something that will be read twice; journalism what will be grasped at once.

CYRIL CONNOLLY (1903–74) British journalist.

61 A good newspaper, I suppose, is a nation talking to itself.

ARTHUR MILLER (1915–) US dramatist.

62 A reporter is a man who has renounced everything in life but the world, the flesh, and the devil.

DAVID MURRAY (1888–1962) British journalist.

63 He's someone who flies around from hotel to hotel and thinks the most interesting thing about any story is the fact that he has arrived to cover it.

TOM STOPPARD (1937–) Czech-born British dramatist. Referring to foreign correspondents

64 There is much to be said in favour of modern journalism. By giving us the opinions of the uneducated, it keeps us in touch with the ignorance of the community.

OSCAR WILDE (1854–1900) Irish-born British dramatist.

Judges

65 The duty of a judge is to administer justice, but his practice is to delay it.

JEAN DE LA BRUYÈRE (1645–96) French satirist.

66 A judge is a law student who marks his own examination papers.

H. L. MENCKEN (1880–1956) US journalist.

67 A judge is not supposed to know anything about the facts of life until they have been presented in evidence and explained to him at least three times.

HUBERT LISTER PARKER (1900–72) Lord Chief Justice of England.

68 Judges, like the criminal classes, have their lighter moments.

OSCAR WILDE (1854–1900) Irish-born British dramatist.

Lawyers

69 A solicitor is a man who calls in a person he doesn't know to sign a contract he hasn't seen to buy property he doesn't want with money he hasn't got.

DINGWALL BATESON (1898–1967) President of the Law Society, 1952–53.

70 There is the prostitute, one who lets out her body for hire. A dreadful thing, but are we ourselves so innocent? Do not lawyers, for instance, let out their brains for hire?

LORD BRABAZON (1884–1964) British motorist, aviator, and politician.

71 If there were no bad people there would be no good lawyers.

CHARLES DICKENS (1812–70) British novelist.

72 God works wonders now and then;
Behold a lawyer, an honest man.

BENJAMIN FRANKLIN (1706–90) US scientist and statesman.

73 Lawyers earn a living by the sweat of their browbeating.

JAMES G. HUNEKER

74 I think we may class the lawyer in the natural history of monsters.

JOHN KEATS (1795–1821) British poet.

75 It is unfair to believe everything we hear about lawyers – some of it might not be true.

GERALD F. LIEBERMAN

76 It has been said that the course to be pursued by a lawyer was first to get on, second to get honour, and third to get honest.

GEORGE M. PALMER

77 A good lawyer is a bad neighbour.

PROVERB

78 A lawyer without history or literature is a mechanic, a mere working mason; if he possesses some knowledge of these, he may venture to call himself an architect.

WALTER SCOTT (1771–1832) Scottish novelist.

Insurance Agents

79 I detest life-insurance agents. They always argue that I shall some day die, which is not so.

STEPHEN LEACOCK (1869–1944) English-born Canadian economist and humorist.

Police

80 I have never seen a situation so dismal that a policeman couldn't make it worse.

BRENDAN BEHAN (1923–64) Irish playwright.

81 I'm not against the police; I'm just afraid of them.

ALFRED HITCHCOCK (1899–1980) British film director.

82 Policemen are numbered in case they get lost.

SPIKE MILLIGAN (1918–   ) British comic actor and author.

83 My father didn't create you to arrest me.

LORD PEEL (1829–1912) British politician.
Protesting against his arrest by the police, recently established by his father

Politicians

84 If a traveller were informed that such a man was leader of the House of Commons, he may well begin to comprehend how the Egyptians worshipped an insect.

BENJAMIN DISRAELI (1804–81) British statesman.
Referring to Lord John Russell

85 When you're abroad you're a statesman: when you're at home you're just a politician.

HAROLD MACMILLAN (1894–1986) British statesman.

86   I used to say that politics was the second lowest profession and I have come to know that it bears a great similarity to the first.

RONALD REAGAN (1911–) US politician and president.

87   Nixon is the kind of politician who would cut down a redwood tree, then mount the stump for a conservation speech.

ADLAI STEVENSON (1900–65) US statesman.

88   Any woman who understands the problems of running a home will be nearer to understanding the problems of running a country.

MARGARET THATCHER (1925–) British politician and prime minister.

89   Politics is the art of preventing people from taking part in affairs which properly concern them.

PAUL VALÉRY (1871–1945) French poet and writer.

90   Any American who is prepared to run for President should automatically, by definition, be disqualified from ever doing so.

GORE VIDAL (1925–) US novelist.

91   Politics come from man. Mercy, compassion and justice come from God.

TERRY WAITE (1939–) British churchman.

Psychiatrists

92   Psychiatrist: A man who asks you a lot of expensive questions your wife asks you for nothing.

SAM BARDELL (1915–   )

93 The trouble with Freud is that he never played the Glasgow Empire Saturday night.

KEN DODD (1931–   ) British comedian.

94 One should only see a psychiatrist out of boredom.

MURIEL SPARK (1918–   ) British novelist.

95 A psychiatrist is a man who goes to the Folies-Bergère and looks at the audience.

MERVYN STOCKWOOD (1913–   ) British churchman.

Servants

96 Here are all kinds of employers wanting all sorts of servants, and all sorts of servants wanting all kinds of employers, and they never seem to come together.

CHARLES DICKENS (1812–70) British novelist.

97 The difference between a man and his valet; they both smoke the same cigars, but only one pays for them.

ROBERT FROST (1875–1963) US poet.

98 A good servant is a real godsend; but truly 'tis a rare bird in the land.

MARTIN LUTHER (1483–1546) German Protestant.

The Services

99 Soldiers in peace are like chimneys in summer.

WILLIAM CECIL, LORD BURGHLEY (1520–98) English statesman.

100 Drinking is the soldier's pleasure.

JOHN DRYDEN (1631–1700) British poet and dramatist.

101 The wonder is always new that any sane man can be a sailor.

RALPH WALDO EMERSON (1803–82) US poet and essayist.

102 No man will be a sailor who has contrivance enough to get himself into a jail; for being in a ship is being in a jail, with the chance of being drowned . . . A man in a jail has more room, better food and commonly better company.

SAMUEL JOHNSON (1709–84) British lexicographer.

103 It's Tommy this, an' Tommy that, an' 'Chuck him out, the brute!'
But it's 'Saviour of 'is country' when the guns begin to shoot.

RUDYARD KIPLING (1865–1936) Indian-born British writer.

104 The worse the man the better the soldier. If soldiers be not corrupt they out to be made so.

NAPOLEON I (Napoleon Bonaparte; 1769–1821) French emperor.

105 When the military man approaches, the world locks up its spoons and packs off its womankind.

GEORGE BERNARD SHAW (1856–1950) Irish dramatist and critic.

106 We sailors get money like horses, and spent it like asses.

TOBIAS SMOLLETT (1721–71) British novelist.

107 He (the recruiting officer) asked me 'Why tanks?' I replied that I preferred to go into battle sitting down.

PETER USTINOV (1921–) British actor.

108 I don't know what effect these men will have on the enemy, but, by God, they frighten me.

DUKE OF WELLINGTON (1769–1852) British general and statesman.
Referring to his generals

Teachers

109 A teacher affects eternity.

HENRY B. ADAMS (1838–1918) US historian.

110 The true teacher defends his pupils against his own personal influence.

A. B. ALCOTT (1799–1888) US writer.

111 Being a professor of poetry is rather like being a Kentucky colonel. It's not really a subject one can profess – unless one hires oneself out to write pieces for funerals or the marriages of dons.

W. H. AUDEN (1907–73) British poet.

112 A schoolmaster should have an atmosphere of awe, and walk wonderingly, as if he was amazed at being himself.

WALTER BAGEHOT (1826–77) British economist and journalist.

113 It were better to perish than to continue schoolmastering.

THOMAS CARLYLE (1795–1881) Scottish historian and essayist.

114 Headmasters have powers at their disposal with which Prime Ministers have never yet been invested.

WINSTON CHURCHILL (1874–1965) British statesman.

115 It is the supreme art of the teacher to awaken joy in creative expression and knowledge.

ALBERT EINSTEIN (1879–1955) German-born US physicist.

116 One looks back with appreciation to the brilliant teachers, but with gratitude to those who touched our human feelings. The curriculum is so much necessary raw material, but warmth is the vital element for the growing plant and for the soul of the child.

CARL GUSTAV JUNG (1875–1961) Swiss psychoanalyst.

117 Therefore for the love of God appoint teachers and schoolmasters, you that have the charge of youth; and give the teachers stipends worthy of the pains.

HUGH LATIMER (1485–1555) English churchman.

118 The average schoolmaster is and always must be essentially an ass, for how can one imagine an intelligent man engaging in so puerile an avocation?

H. L. MENCKEN (1880–1956) US journalist.

119 A teacher is one who, in his youth, admired teachers.

H. L. MENCKEN

120 I am inclined to think that one's education has been in vain if one fails to learn that most schoolmasters are idiots.

HESKETH PEARSON (1887–1964) British biographer.

121 A teacher should have maximal authority and minimal power.

THOMAS SZASZ (1920–) US psychiatrist.

OPPORTUNITY

1 Opportunities are usually disguised as hard work, so most people don't recognise them.

ANN LANDERS (1918–) US journalist.

2 One can present people with opportunities. One cannot make them equal to them.

ROSAMOND LEHMANN (1901–90) British novelist.

3 Equality of opportunity means equal opportunity to be unequal.

IAIN MACLEOD (1913–70) British politician.

OPTIMISM

1 The optimist proclaims we live in the best of all possible worlds; and the pessimist fears this is true.

JAMES CABELL (1879–1958) US novelist and journalist.

2   The latest definition of an optimist is one who fills up his crossword puzzle in ink.

    CLEMENT KING SHORTER (1857–1926) British journalist and critic.

3   I am an optimist, unrepentant and militant. After all, in order not to be a fool an optimist must know how sad a place the world can be. It is only the pessimist who finds this out anew every day.

    PETER USTINOV (1921–) British actor.

PARTIES

1   I entertained on a cruising trip that was so much fun that I had to sink my yacht to make my guests go home.

    F. SCOTT FITZGERALD (1896–1940) US novelist.

2   The best number for a dinner party is two – myself and a dam' good head waiter.

    NUBAR GULBENKIAN (1896–1972) Turkish oil magnate.

3   Certainly, there is nothing else here to enjoy.

    GEORGE BERNARD SHAW (1856–1950) Irish dramatist and critic.
    Said at a party when his hostess asked him whether he was enjoying himself

PAST

1   We are always doing something for posterity, but I would fain see posterity do something for us.

    JOSEPH ADDISON (1672–1719) British essayist.

2   Even God cannot change the past.

   AGATHON (c. 446–401 BC) Athenian poet and playwright.

3   The past is a foreign country: they do things differently there.

   L. P. HARTLEY (1895–1972) British novelist.

4   Look back, and smile at perils past.

   WALTER SCOTT (1771–1832) Scottish novelist.

5   The past is the only dead thing that smells sweet.

   EDWARD THOMAS (1878–1917) British poet.

6   Keep off your thoughts from things that are past and done;
   For thinking of the past wakes regret and pain.

   ARTHUR WALEY (1889–1966) British poet and translator.
   Translation from the Chinese of Po-Chü-I

7   The past, at least, is secure.

   DANIEL WEBSTER (1782–1852) US statesman.

PATRIOTISM

1   Our country! In her intercourse with foreign nations, may she always be in the right; but our country, right or wrong.

   STEPHEN DECATUR (1779–1820) US naval officer.

2   Patriotism is the last refuge of a scoundrel.

   SAMUEL JOHNSON (1709–84) British lexicographer.

PEACE

1   *Peace,* n. In international affairs, a period of cheating between two periods of fighting.

AMBROSE BIERCE (1842–?1914) US writer and journalist.

2   Arms alone are not enough to keep the peace – it must be kept by men.

JOHN FITZGERALD KENNEDY (1917–63) US statesman.

3   The issues are the same. We wanted peace on earth, love, and understanding between everyone around the world. We have learned that change comes slowly.

PAUL MCCARTNEY (1943–) British rock musician.

PERFECTION

1   Perfection has one grave defect; it is apt to be dull.

W. SOMERSET MAUGHAM (1874–1965) British novelist.

PESSIMISM

1   The optimist proclaims we live in the best of all possible worlds; and the pessimist fears this is true.

JAMES CABELL (1879–1958) US novelist and journalist.

2   If we see light at the end of the tunnel it is the light of an oncoming train.

ROBERT LOWELL (1917–77) US poet.

PLACES

1   There are few more impressive sights in the world than a Scotsman on the make.

J. M. BARRIE (1860–1937) British novelist and dramatist.

2   Streets full of water. Please advise.

ROBERT BENCHLEY (1889–1945) US humorist.
Telegram sent to his editor on arriving in Venice

3   England is a paradise for women, and hell for horses: Italy a paradise for horses, hell for women.

ROBERT BURTON (1577–1640) English scholar and explorer.

4   Well, the principle seems the same. The water still keeps falling over.

WINSTON CHURCHILL (1874–1965) British statesman.
When asked whether the Niagara Falls looked the same as when he first saw them

5   The Almighty in His infinite wisdom did not see fit to create Frenchmen in the image of Englishmen.

WINSTON CHURCHILL

6   India is a geographical term. It is no more a united nation than the Equator.

WINSTON CHURCHILL

7   I cannot forecast to you the action of Russia. It is a riddle wrapped in a mystery inside an enigma.

WINSTON CHURCHILL

8   There are many things in life more worthwhile than money. One is to be brought up in this our England which is still the envy of less happy lands.

LORD DENNING (1899–) British judge.

9   Latins are tenderly enthusiastic. In Brazil they throw flowers at you. In Argentina they throw themselves.

MARLENE DIETRICH (Maria Magdalene von Losch; 1904–92) German-born film star.

10   If you are lucky enough to have lived in Paris as a young man, then wherever you go for the rest of your life, it stays with you, for Paris is a moveable feast.

ERNEST HEMINGWAY (1899–1961) US novelist.

11   Dublin, though a place much worse than London, is not so bad as Iceland.

SAMUEL JOHNSON (1709–84) British lexicographer.
Letter to Mrs Christopher Smart

12   Much may be made of a Scotchman, if he be *caught* young.

SAMUEL JOHNSON
Referring to Lord Mansfield

13   Their learning is like bread in a besieged town: every man gets a little, but no man gets a full meal.

SAMUEL JOHNSON
Referring to education in Scotland

14   An Englishman, even if he is alone, forms an orderly queue of one.

GEORGE MIKES (1912–87) Hungarian-born British writer.

15 Continental people have sex life; the English have hot-water bottles.

GEORGE MIKES

16 Remember that you are an Englishman, and have consequently won first prize in the lottery of life.

CECIL RHODES (1853–1902) South African statesman.

17 The English have no respect for their language, and will not teach their children to speak it . . . It is impossible for an Englishman to open his mouth, without making some other Englishman despise him.

GEORGE BERNARD SHAW (1856–1950) Irish dramatist and critic.

18 Cusins is a very nice fellow, certainly: nobody would ever guess that he was born in Australia.

GEORGE BERNARD SHAW

19 There are still parts of Wales where the only concession to gaiety is a striped shroud.

GWYN THOMAS (1913–81) British writer.

20 Men of England! You wish to kill me because I am a Frenchman. Am I not punished enough in not being born an Englishman?

VOLTAIRE (François-Marie Arouet; 1694–1778) French writer.
Addressing an angry London mob who desired to hang him because he was a Frenchman

21 You never find an Englishman among the underdogs – except in England of course.

EVELYN WAUGH (1903–66) British novelist.

22 It is never difficult to distinguish between a Scotsman with a grievance and a ray of sunshine.

P. G. WODEHOUSE (1881–1975) British humorous novelist.

PLEASURE

1 One half of the world cannot understand the pleasures of the other.

JANE AUSTEN (1775–1817) British novelist.

2 All the things I really like to do are either immoral, illegal, or fattening.

ALEXANDER WOOLLCOTT (1887–1943) US journalist.

POPULARITY

1 Everybody hates me because I'm so universally liked.

PETER DE VRIES (1910–   ) US novelist.

2 He hasn't an enemy in the world, and none of his friends like him.

OSCAR WILDE (1854–1900) Irish-born British dramatist. Said of G. B. Shaw

POVERTY

1   It is only the poor who are forbidden to beg.

ANATOLE FRANCE (Jacques Anatole François Thibault; 1844–1924) French writer.

2   Look at me: I worked my way up from nothing to a state of extreme poverty.

GROUCHO MARX (Julius Marx; 1895–1977) US comedian.

3   Whereas it has long been known and declared that the poor have no right to the property of the rich, I wish it also to be known and declared that the rich have no right to the property of the poor.

JOHN RUSKIN (1819–1900) British art critic and writer.

4   When the rich wage war it is the poor who die.

JEAN-PAUL SARTRE (1905–80) French writer.

5   There were times my pants were so thin I could sit on a dime and tell if it was heads or tails.

SPENCER TRACY (1900–67) US film star.

POWER

1   Power tends to corrupt, and absolute power corrupts absolutely. Great men are almost always bad men . . . There is no worse heresy than that the office sanctifies the holder of it.

LORD ACTON (1834–1902) British historian.
Often misquoted as 'Power corrupts . . . '

2 He did not care in which direction the car was travelling, so long as he remained in the driver's seat.

   LORD BEAVERBROOK (1879–1964) Canadian-born British newspaper proprietor.
   Referring to Lloyd George

3 There is one thing about being President – nobody can tell you when to sit down.

   DWIGHT D. EISENHOWER (1890–1969) US general and statesman.

4 Men of power have not time to read; yet men who do not read are unfit for power.

   MICHAEL FOOT (1913–   ) British Labour politician and journalist.

5 You only have power over people so long as you don't take *everything* away from them. But when you've robbed a man of everything he's no longer in your power – he's free again.

   ALEXANDER SOLZHENITSYN (1918–   ) Soviet novelist.

6 God is always on the side of the big battalions.

   VICOMTE DE TURENNE (1611–75) French marshal.

7 God is on the side not of the heavy battalions, but of the best shots.

   VOLTAIRE (François-Marie Arouet; 1694–1778) French writer.

8 The wrong sort of people are always in power because they would not be in power if they were not the wrong sort of people.

   JON WYNNE-TYSON (1924–   ) British humorous writer.

PRACTICALITY

1   Don't carry away that arm till I have taken off my ring.

    LORD RAGLAN (1788–1855) British field marshal.
    Request immediately after his arm had been amputated following the battle of Waterloo

2   Very well, then I shall not take off my boots.

    DUKE OF WELLINGTON (1769–1852) British general and statesman.
    Responding to the news, as he was going to bed, that the ship in which he was travelling seemed about to sink

PRAISE

1   The advantage of doing one's praising for oneself is that one can lay it on so thick and exactly in the right places.

    SAMUEL BUTLER (1835–1902) British writer.

2   To refuse praise reveals a desire to be praised twice over.

    DUC DE LA ROCHEFOUCAULD (1613–80) French writer.

PRAYER

1   The idea that He would take his attention away from the universe in order to give me a bicycle with three speeds is just so unlikely I can't go along with it.

    QUENTIN CRISP (?1910–) British model, publicist, and writer.

2   Forgive, O Lord, my little jokes on Thee

And I'll forgive Thy great big one on me.

ROBERT FROST (1875–1963) US poet.

3 I am just going to pray for you at St Paul's, but with no very lively hope of success.

SYDNEY SMITH (1771–1845) British clergyman and essayist.
On meeting an acquaintance

PREJUDICE

1 Common sense is the collection of prejudices acquired by age eighteen.

ALBERT EINSTEIN (1879–1955) German-born US physicist.

PRESENT

1 Gather ye rosebuds while ye may,
Old time is still a-flying:
And this same flower that smiles today
Tomorrow will be dying.

ROBERT HERRICK (1591–1674) English poet.

2 Drop the question what tomorrow may bring, and count as profit every day that Fate allows you.

HORACE (Quintus Horatius Flaccus; 65–8 BC) Roman poet.

PRINCIPLES

1 It is easier to fight for one's principles than to live up to them.

ALFRED ADLER (1870–1937) Austrian psychiatrist.

2   Whenever two good people argue over principles, they are both right.

MARIE EBNER VON ESCHENBACH (1830–1916) Austrian writer.

3   Nobody ever did anything very foolish except from some strong principle.

LORD MELBOURNE (1779–1848) British statesman.

PROGRESS

1   The people who live in the past must yield to the people who live in the future. Otherwise the world would begin to turn the other way round.

ARNOLD BENNETT (1867–1931) British novelist.

2   All progress is based upon a universal innate desire on the part of every organism to live beyond its income.

SAMUEL BUTLER (1835–1902) British writer.

3   What we call progress is the exchange of one nuisance for another nuisance.

HAVELOCK ELLIS (1859–1939) British sexologist.

4   All that is human must retrograde if it does not advance.

EDWARD GIBBON (1737–94) British historian.

5   You cannot fight against the future. Time is on our side.

WILLIAM EWART GLADSTONE (1809–98) British statesman.
Advocating parliamentary reform

6   If I have seen further it is by standing on the shoulders of giants.

ISAAC NEWTON (1642–1727) British scientist.

PROMISES

1   Better is it that thou shouldest not vow, than that thou shouldest vow and not pay.

BIBLE: ECCLESIASTES

2   A promise made is a debt unpaid.

ROBERT WILLIAM SERVICE (1874–1958) Canadian poet.

PROMPTNESS

1   Punctuality is the politeness of kings.

LOUIS XVIII (1755–1824) French king.

2   Punctuality is the virtue of the bored.

EVELYN WAUGH (1903–66) British novelist.

PRONUNCIATION

1   Everybody has a right to pronounce foreign names as he chooses.

WINSTON CHURCHILL (1874–1965) British statesman.

PROPHECY

1   Mr Turnbull had predicted evil consequences . . .
    and was now doing the best in his power to bring
    about the verification of his own prophecies.

    ANTHONY TROLLOPE (1815–82) British novelist.

PUBLIC

1   You cannot make a man by standing a sheep on its
    hind legs. But by standing a flock of sheep in that
    position you can make a crowd of men.

    MAX BEERBOHM (1872–1956) British writer.

2   The Public is an old woman. Let her maunder and
    mumble.

    THOMAS CARLYLE (1795–1881) Scottish historian and
    essayist.

3   The people would be just as noisy if they were going
    to see me hanged.

    OLIVER CROMWELL (1599–1658) English soldier and
    statesman.
    Referring to a cheering crowd

4   There is not a more mean, stupid, dastardly, pitiful,
    selfish, spiteful, envious, ungrateful animal than the
    public. It is the greatest of cowards, for it is afraid
    of itself.

    WILLIAM HAZLITT (1778–1830) British essayist.

5   Only constant repetition will finally succeed in im-
    printing an idea on the memory of the crowd.

    ADOLF HITLER (1889–1945) German dictator.

6   The people long eagerly for just two things – bread and circuses.

   JUVENAL   (Decimus Junius Juvenalis; 60–130 AD)   Roman satirist.

PURITY

1   I'm as pure as the driven slush.

   TALLULAH BANKHEAD   (1903–68)   US actress.

2   Caesar's wife must be above suspicion.

   PROVERB

3   It is one of the superstitions of the human mind to have imagined that virginity could be a virtue.

   VOLTAIRE   (François-Marie Arouet; 1694–1778)   French writer.

4   I used to be Snow White . . . but I drifted.

   MAE WEST   (1892–1980)   US actress.

REGRET

1   Were it not better to forget
Than but remember and regret?

   LETITIA LANDON   (1802–38)   British poet and novelist.

2   The follies which a man regrets most in his life are those which he didn't commit when he had the opportunity.

   HELEN ROWLAND   (1876–1950)   US writer.

3   What's gone and what's past help
      Should be past grief.

WILLIAM SHAKESPEARE (1564–1616) English dramatist.

RELIGION

1   The Jews and Arabs should sit down and settle their
      differences like good Christians.

WARREN AUSTIN (1877–1962) US politician and diplomat.

2   The idea that only a male can represent Christ at the
      altar is a most serious heresy.

DR GEORGE CAREY (1935–   ) British churchman and Archbishop of Canterbury (1991–   ).

3   There exists no politician in India daring enough to
      attempt to explain to the masses that cows can be
      eaten.

INDIRA GANDHI (1917–84) Indian stateswoman.

4   When the white man came we had the land and they
      had the Bibles; now they have the land and we have
      the Bibles.

DAN GEORGE (1899–1982) Canadian Indian chief.

REPUTATION

1   I hold it as certain, that no man was ever written out
      of reputation but by himself.

RICHARD BENTLEY (1662–1742) English academic.

2   Until you've lost your reputation, you never realize what a burden it was or what freedom really is.

MARGARET MITCHELL (1909–49) US novelist.

RESPONSIBILITY

1   Perhaps it is better to be irresponsible and right than to be responsible and wrong.

WINSTON CHURCHILL (1874–1965) British statesman.

2   The buck stops here.

HARRY S. TRUMAN (1884–1972) US statesman.
Sign kept on his desk during his term as president

RIDICULE

1   Few women care to be laughed at and men not at all, except for large sums of money.

ALAN AYCKBOURN (1939–   ) British dramatist.

RIGHT

1   This the grave of Mike O'Day
Who died maintaining his right of way.
His right was clear, his will was strong.
But he's just as dead as if he'd been wrong.

ANONYMOUS

ROYALTY

1   Her Majesty is not a subject.

BENJAMIN DISRAELI (1804–81) British statesman.
Responding to Gladstone's taunt that Disraeli could make
a joke out of any subject, including Queen Victoria

2 It has none, your Highness. Its history dates from
today.

JAMES WHISTLER (1834–1903) US painter.
Replying to a query from the Prince of Wales about the
history of the Society of British Artists, which he was
visiting for the first time

RUTHLESSNESS

1 We are programmed (by biology or conditioning –
who cares which?) to respond to social signals and
pressures, and so find it almost impossible to be as
single-mindedly ruthless as men.

JANET DALEY   British journalist.

2 I do not have to forgive my enemies, I have had
them all shot.

RAMÓN MARIA NARVÁEZ (1800–68) Spanish general and
political leader.
Said on his deathbed, when asked by a priest if he for-
gave his enemies

3 It is not enough to succeed. Others must fail.

GORE VIDAL (1925–) US novelist.

SARCASM

1 If you don't want to use the army, I should like to
   borrow it for a while. Yours respectfully, A. Lincoln.

   ABRAHAM LINCOLN (1809–65) US statesman.
   Letter to General George B. McClellan, whose lack of
   activity during the US Civil War irritated Lincoln

SCIENCE

1 It is, of course, a bit of a drawback that science was
   invented after I left school.

   LORD CARRINGTON (1919–   ) British statesman.

2 When you are courting a nice girl an hour seems like
   a second. When you sit on a red-hot cinder a second
   seems like an hour. That's relativity.

   ALBERT EINSTEIN (1879–1955) German-born US
   physicist.

3 The airplane stays up because it doesn't have the
   time to fall.

   ORVILLE WRIGHT (1871–1948) US aviator.
   Explaining the principles of powered flight

SELF-CONTROL

1 When things are steep, remember to stay level-
   headed.

   HORACE (Quintus Horatius Flaccus; 65–8 BC) Roman
   poet.

2 If you can keep your head when all about you
   Are losing theirs and blaming it on you.

RUDYARD KIPLING (1865–1936) Indian-born British writer.

SELFLESSNESS

1   To give and not to count the cost;
To fight and not to heed the wounds;
To toil and not to seek for rest;
To labour and not ask for any reward
Save that of knowing that we do Thy will.

St Ignatius Loyola (1491–1556) Spanish priest.

SELF-MADE MEN

1   I know he is, and he adores his maker.

Benjamin Disraeli (1804–81) British statesman.
Replying to a remark made in defence of John Bright
that he was a self-made man

2   He was a self-made man who owed his lack of success to nobody.

Joseph Heller (1923–) US novelist.

3   A self-made man is one who believes in luck and sends his son to Oxford.

Christina Stead (1902–83) Australian novelist.

SELF-PRESERVATION

1   This animal is very bad; when attacked it defends itself.

Anonymous

SERIOUSNESS

1   Angels can fly because they take themselves lightly.

G. K. CHESTERTON (1874–1936) British writer.

SEX

1   My brain: it's my second favourite organ.

WOODY ALLEN (Allen Stewart Konigsberg; 1935–   ) US film actor.

2   It was the most fun I ever had without laughing.

WOODY ALLEN

3   Money, it turned out, was exactly like sex, you thought of nothing else if you didn't have it and thought of other things if you did.

JAMES BALDWIN (1924–87) US writer.

4   When she raises her eyelids it's as if she were taking off all her clothes.

COLETTE (1873–1954) French novelist.

5   I see – she's the original good time that was had by all.

BETTE DAVIS (Ruth Elizabeth Davis; 1908–89) US film star. Referring to a starlet of the time

6   Personally I know nothing about sex because I've always been married.

ZSA ZSA GABOR (1919–   ) Hungarian-born US film star.

7   Sexual intercourse began
    In nineteen sixty-three
    (Which was rather late for me) –

Between the end of the *Chatterley* ban
And the Beatles' first LP.

PHILIP LARKIN (1922–85) British poet.

8   You know, she speaks eighteen languages. And she can't say 'No' in any of them.

DOROTHY PARKER (1893–1967) US writer.
Speaking of an acquaintance

9   I'm glad you like my Catherine. I like her too. She ruled thirty million people and had three thousand lovers. I do the best I can in two hours.

MAE WEST (1892–1980) US actress.
After her performance in *Catherine the Great*

10 It's not the men in my life that count; it's the life in my men.

MAE WEST

11 When I'm good I'm very good, but when I'm bad I'm better.

MAE WEST

SIMPLICITY

1   A child of five would understand this.
Send somebody to fetch a child of five.

GROUCHO MARX (Julius Marx; 1895–1977) US comedian.

SINCERITY

1   What comes from the heart, goes to the heart.

SAMUEL TAYLOR COLERIDGE (1772–1834) British poet.

2   I'm afraid of losing my obscurity. Genuineness only
     thrives in the dark. Like celery.

     ALDOUS HUXLEY (1894–1964) British novelist.

3   What's a man's first duty? The answer's brief: To be
     himself.

     HENRIK IBSEN (1828–1906) Norwegian dramatist.

SLEEP

1   Laugh and the world laughs with you; snore and you
     sleep alone.

     ANTHONY BURGESS (1917–   ) British novelist and critic.

SMOKING

1   Certainly not – if you don't object if I'm sick.

     THOMAS BEECHAM (1879–1961) British conductor.
     When asked whether he minded if someone smoked in a
     non-smoking compartment

2   I must point out that my rule of life prescribed as an
     absolutely sacred rite smoking cigars and also the
     drinking of alcohol before, after, and if need be dur-
     ing all meals and in the intervals between them.

     WINSTON CHURCHILL (1874–1965) British statesman.
     Said during a lunch with the Arab leader Ibn Saud, when
     he heard that the king's religion forbade smoking and
     alcohol

3   A custom loathsome to the eye, hateful to the nose, harmful to the brain, dangerous to the lungs, and in the black, stinking fume thereof, nearest resembling the horrible Stygian smoke of the pit that is bottomless.

JAMES I (1566–1625) King of England.

4   He who lives without tobacco is not worthy to live.

MOLIÈRE (Jean Baptiste Poquelin; 1622–73) French dramatist.

5   This vice brings in one hundred million francs in taxes every year. I will certainly forbid it at once – as soon as you can name a virtue that brings in as much revenue.

NAPOLEON III (1808–73) French emperor.
Reply when asked to ban smoking

SNOBBERY

1   Of course they have, or I wouldn't be sitting here talking to someone like you.

BARBARA CARTLAND (1902–) British romantic novelist.
When asked in a radio interview whether she thought that British class barriers had broken down

2   I mustn't go on singling out names. One must not be a name-dropper, as Her Majesty remarked to me yesterday.

NORMAN ST JOHN STEVAS (1929–) British politician.

3   She was – but I assure you that she was a very bad cook.

LOUIS ADOLPHE THIERS (1797–1877) French statesman and historian.
Defending his social status after someone had remarked that his mother had been a cook

SORROW

1   One often calms one's grief by recounting it.

PIERRE CORNEILLE (1606–84) French dramatist.

2   The secret of being miserable is to have leisure to bother about whether you are happy or not.

GEORGE BERNARD SHAW (1856–1950) Irish dramatist and critic.

SPEECH

1   *Bore*, n. A person who talks when you wish him to listen.

AMBROSE BIERCE (1842–?1914) US writer and journalist.

2   Oaths are but words, and words but wind.

SAMUEL BUTLER (1612–80) English satirist.

3   When you have nothing to say, say nothing.

CHARLES CALEB COLTON (?1780–1832) British clergyman and writer.

4   No, Sir, because I have time to think before I speak, and don't ask impertinent questions.

ERASMUS DARWIN (1731–1802) British physician, biologist, and poet.

Reply when asked whether he found his stammer
inconvenient

5   You can stroke people with words.

F. SCOTT FITZGERALD (1896–1940) US novelist.

6   The true use of speech is not so much to express
    our wants as to conceal them.

OLIVER GOLDSMITH (1728–74) Irish-born British writer.

7   Most men make little use of their speech than to
    give evidence against their own understanding.

LORD HALIFAX (1633–95) English statesman.

8   That man's silence is wonderful to listen to.

THOMAS HARDY (1840–1928) British novelist.

9   Silence is as full of potential wisdom and wit as the
    unhewn marble of great sculpture.

ALDOUS HUXLEY (1894–1964) British novelist.

10 Talking and eloquence are not the same: to speak,
    and to speak well, are two things.

BEN JONSON (1573–1637) English dramatist.

11 Words are, of course, the most powerful drug used
    by mankind.

RUDYARD KIPLING (1865–1936) Indian-born British
writer.

12 Beware of the conversationalist who adds 'in other
    words'. He is merely starting afresh.

ROBERT MORLEY (1908–) British actor.

13 The most precious things in speech are pauses.

RALPH RICHARDSON (1902–83) British actor.

14 But words once spoke can never be recall'd.

EARL OF ROSCOMMON (1633–85) Irish-born English poet.

15 He has occasional flashes of silence, that make his conversation perfectly delightful.

SYDNEY SMITH (1771–1845) British clergyman and essayist.
Referring to Lord Macaulay

16 A good listener is not someone who has nothing to say. A good listener is a good talker with a sore throat.

KATHERINE WHITEHORN (1926–   ) British journalist.

SPORT

1 Golf is a game whose aim is to hit a very small ball into an even smaller hole, with weapons singularly ill-designed for the purpose.

WINSTON CHURCHILL (1874–1965) British statesman.

2 Exercise is bunk. If you are healthy, you don't need it: if you are sick, you shouldn't take it.

HENRY FORD (1863–1947) US car manufacturer.

3 They came to see me bat not to see you bowl.

W. G. GRACE (1848–1915) British doctor and cricketer.
Refusing to leave the crease after being bowled first ball in front of a large crowd

4 It's more than a game. It's an institution.

SMALLCAPS THOMAS HUGHES (1822–96) British novelist.
Referring to cricket

5 Casting a ball at three straight sticks and defending the same with a fourth.

RUDYARD KIPLING (1865–1936) Indian-born British writer.

6 Golf may be played on Sunday, not being a game within the view of the law, but being a form of moral effort.

STEPHEN LEACOCK (1869–1944) English-born Canadian economist and humorist.

7 All I've got against it is that it takes you so far from the club house.

ERIC LINKLATER (1889–1974) Scottish novelist.
Referring to golf

8 It is almost impossible to remember how tragic a place the world is when one is playing golf.

ROBERT LYND (1879–1949) Irish essayist and journalist.

9 Football isn't a matter of life and death – it's much more important than that.

BILL SHANKLY (1914–81) British football manager.

10 I have always looked upon cricket as organised loafing.

WILLIAM TEMPLE (1881–1944) British churchman.
Address to parents when headmaster of Repton School

11 Golf is a good walk spoiled.

MARK TWAIN (Samuel Langhorne Clemens; 1835–1910) US writer.

12   There's no secret. You just press the accelerator to the floor and steer left.

BILL VUKOVICH (1918–55) US motor-racing driver. Explaining his success in the Indianapolis 500

13   It requires one to assume such indecent postures.

OSCAR WILDE (1854–1900) Irish-born British dramatist. Explaining why he did not play cricket

14   A day spent in a round of strenuous idleness.

WILLIAM WORDSWORTH (1770–1850) British poet.

SUCCESS

1   The penalty of success is to be bored by people who used to snub you.

NANCY ASTOR (1879–1964) American-born British politician.

2   The shortest and best way to make your fortune is to let people see clearly that it is in their interests to promote yours.

JEAN DE LA BRUYÈRE (1645–96) French satirist.

3   The reward of a thing well done is to have done it.

RALPH WALDO EMERSON (1803–82) US poet and essayist.

4   The only place where success comes before work is a dictionary.

VIDAL SASSOON (1928–   ) British hair stylist.

5   There are no gains without pains.

ADLAI STEVENSON (1900–65) US statesman.

SUPERSTITION

1   Of course I don't believe in it. But I understand that it brings you luck whether you believe in it or not.

NIELS BOHR (1885–1962) Danish physicist.
When asked why he had a horseshoe on his wall

2   I am a great believer in luck, and I find the harder I work the more I have of it.

STEPHEN LEACOCK (1869–1944) English-born Canadian economist and humorist.

SUPPORT

1   What I want is men who will support me when I am in the wrong.

LORD MELBOURNE (1779–1848) British statesman.
Replying to someone who said he would support Melbourne as long as he was in the right

SURVIVAL

1   I haven't asked you to make me young again. All I want is to go cn getting older.

KONRAD ADENAUER (1876–1967) German statesman.
Replying to his doctor

TAXATION

1   Sir, I now pay you this exorbitant charge, but I must ask you to explain to her Majesty that she must not in future look upon me as a source of income.

CHARLES KEMBLE (1775–1854) British actor.
On being obliged to hand over his income tax to the tax collector

TECHNOLOGY

1   What is the use of a new-born child?

BENJAMIN FRANKLIN (1706–90) US scientist and statesman.
Response when asked the same question of a new invention

2   One machine can do the work of fifty ordinary men. No machine can do the work of one extraordinary man.

ELBERT HUBBARD (1856–1915) US writer.

TEMPTATION

1   I never resist temptation because I have found that things that are bad for me never tempt me.

GEORGE BERNARD SHAW (1856–1950) Irish dramatist and critic.

2   The only way to get rid of a temptation is to yield to it.

OSCAR WILDE (1854–1900) Irish-born British dramatist.
Repeating a similar sentiment expressed by Clementina Stirling Graham (1782–1877)

THEATRE

1 You know, I go to the theatre to be entertained . . .
   I don't want to see plays about rape, sodomy and
   drug addiction . . . I can get all that at home.

   PETER COOK (1937–   ) British writer and entertainer.

THINKING

1 The most fluent talkers or most plausible reasoners
   are not always the justest thinkers.

   WILLIAM HAZLITT (1778–1830) British essayist.

2 You can't think rationally on an empty stomach, and
   a whole lot of people can't do it on a full one either.

   LORD REITH (1889–1971) British administrator.

TIME

1 The Future is something which everyone reaches at
   the rate of sixty minutes an hour, whatever he does,
   whoever he is.

   C. S. LEWIS (1898–1963) British academic and writer.

TRUST

1 We are inclined to believe those whom we do not
   know because they have never deceived us.

   SAMUEL JOHNSON (1709–84) British lexicographer.

TRUTH

1   The truth that makes men free is for the most part the truth which men prefer not to hear.

HERBERT SEBASTIAN AGAR (1897–1980) US writer.

2   And ye shall know the truth, and the truth shall make you free.

BIBLE: JOHN

3   Some men love truth so much that they seem to be in continual fear lest she should catch a cold on overexposure.

SAMUEL BUTLER (1835–1902) British writer.

4   It is an old maxim of mine that when you have excluded the impossible, whatever remains, however improbable, must be the truth.

ARTHUR CONAN DOYLE (1856–1930) British writer.

5   Truth, like a torch, the more it's shook it shines.

WILLIAM HAMILTON (1788–1856) Scottish philosopher.

6   There are no new truths, but only truths that have not been recognized by those who have perceived them without noticing.

MARY MCCARTHY (1912–89) US novelist.

7   It takes two to speak the truth – one to speak, and another to hear.

HENRY DAVID THOREAU (1817–62) US writer.

UNCERTAINTY

1 Of course not. After all, I may be wrong.

BERTRAND RUSSELL (1872–1970) British philosopher.
On being asked whether he would be prepared to die for
his beliefs

UNDERSTANDING

1 I used to tell my husband that, if he could make *me*
understand something, it would be clear to all the
other people in the country.

ELEANOR ROOSEVELT (1884–1962) US writer and
lecturer.

UNIVERSE

1 Had I been present at the Creation, I would have
given some useful hints for the better ordering of
the universe.

ALFONSO THE WISE (c. 1221–84) King of Castile and
Léon.
Referring to the complicated Ptolemaic model of the universe. Often quoted as, 'Had I been consulted I would
have recommended something simpler'.

VERBOSITY

1 I have made this letter longer than usual, only because I have not had the time to make it shorter.

BLAISE PASCAL (1623–62) French philosopher and
mathematician.

VICE

1   Whenever I'm caught between two evils, I take the one I've never tried.

    MAE WEST (1892–1980) US actress.

VIRTUE

1   To be able to practise five things everywhere under heaven constitutes perfect virtue . . . gravity, generosity of soul, sincerity, earnestness, and kindness.

    CONFUCIUS (K'ung Fu-tzu; 551–479 BC) Chinese philosopher.

WEAPONS

1   It was very successful, but it fell on the wrong planet.

    WERNHER VON BRAUN (1912–77) German rocket engineer.
    Referring to the first V2 rocket to hit London during World War II

WEDDINGS

1   If it were not for the presents, an elopement would be preferable.

    GEORGE ADE (1866–1944) US dramatist and humorist.

2   It is a truth universally acknowledged, that a single man in possession of a good fortune must be in want of a wife.

    JANE AUSTEN (1775–1817) British novelist.

The opening words of *Pride and Prejudice*

3 Wives are young men's mistresses, companions for middle age, and old men's nurses.

FRANCIS BACON (1561–1626) English philosopher.

4 He was reputed one of the wise men, that made answer to the question, when a man should marry? A young man not yet, an elder man not at all.

FRANCIS BACON

5 It is easier to be a lover than a husband, for the same reason that it is more difficult to show a ready wit all day long than to produce an occasional *bon mot.*

HONORÉ DE BALZAC (1799–1850) French novelist.

6 Let the husband render unto the wife due benevolence: and likewise also the wife unto the husband.

BIBLE: I CORINTHIANS

7 But if they cannot contain, let them marry: for it is better to marry than to burn.

BIBLE: I CORINTHIANS

8 Ah, gentle dames! It gars me greet
To think how mony counsels sweet,
How mony lengthen'd sage advices,
The husband frae the wife despises!

ROBERT BURNS (1759–96) Scottish poet.

9 An archaeologist is the best husband any woman can have: the older she gets, the more interested he is in her.

AGATHA CHRISTIE (1891–1976) British detective-story writer.

10 Marriage is a wonderful invention; but then again so is a bicycle repair kit.

BILLY CONNOLLY (1942–   ) British comedian.

11 Husbands are like fires. They go out when unattended.

ZSA ZSA GABOR (1919–   ) Hungarian-born US film star.

12 The concept of two people living together for 25 years without having a cross word suggests a lack of spirit only to be admired in sheep.

A. P. HERBERT (1890–1971) British writer and politican.

13 The triumph of hope over experience.

SAMUEL JOHNSON (1709–84) British lexicographer. Referring to the hasty remarriage of an acquaintance following the death of his first wife, with whom he had been most unhappy

14 Love is moral even without legal marriage, but marriage is immoral without love.

ELLEN KEY (Karolina Sofia Key; 1849–1926) Swedish writer.

15 It has been said that a bride's attitude towards her betrothed can be summed up in three words: Aisle. Altar. Hymn.

FRANK MUIR (1920–   ) British writer and broadcaster.

16 Strange to say what delight we married people have to see these poor fools decoyed into our condition.

SAMUEL PEPYS (1633–1703) English diarist.

17 It doesn't much signify whom one marries, for one is sure to find next morning that it was someone else.

SAMUEL ROGERS (1763–1855) British poet.

18 Never trust a husband too far, nor a bachelor too near.

HELEN ROWLAND (1876–1950) US writer.

19 It takes two to make a marriage a success and only one a failure.

HERBERT SAMUEL (1870–1963) British Liberal statesman.

20 Marriage is popular because it combines the maximum of temptation with the maximum of opportunity.

GEORGE BERNARD SHAW (1856–1950) Irish dramatist and critic.

21 Remember, it is as easy to marry a rich woman as a poor woman.

WILLIAM MAKEPEACE THACKERAY (1811–63) British novelist.

22 Marriage is the only adventure open to the cowardly.

VOLTAIRE (François-Marie Arouet; 1694–1778) French writer.

23 LORD ILLINGWORTH. The Book of Life begins with a man and a woman in a garden.
MRS ALLONBY. It ends with Revelations.

OSCAR WILDE (1854–1900) Irish-born British dramatist.

24 A man looks pretty small at a wedding, George. All those good women standing shoulder to shoulder, making sure that the knot's tied in a mighty public way.

THORNTON WILDER (1897–1975) US novelist and dramatist.

WISDOM

1 For in much wisdom is much grief: and he that increaseth knowledge increaseth sorrow.

BIBLE: ECCLESIASTES

2 Be wiser than other people if you can, but do not tell them so.

EARL OF CHESTERFIELD (1694–1773) English statesman.

3 It is the province of knowledge to speak and it is the privilege of wisdom to listen.

OLIVER WENDELL HOLMES (1809–94) US writer.

WOMEN

1 A woman seldom asks advice until she has bought her wedding clothes.

JOSEPH ADDISON (1672–1719) British essayist.

2 One is not born a woman, one becomes one.

SIMONE DE BEAUVOIR (1908–86) French writer.

3 Most women are not so young as they are painted.

MAX BEERBOHM (1872–1956) British writer.

4 Brigands demand your money or your life; women require both.

SAMUEL BUTLER (1835–1902) British writer.

5 Wherever one wants to be kissed.

COCO CHANEL (1883–1971) French dress designer.
When asked where one should wear perfume

6 I should like to know what is the proper function of women, if it is not to make reasons for husbands to stay at home, and still stronger reasons for bachelors to go out.

GEORGE ELIOT (Mary Ann Evans; 1819–80) British novelist.

7 When a woman behaves like a man, why doesn't she behave like a nice man?

EDITH EVANS (1888–1976) British actress.

8 My mother said it was simple to keep a man, you must be a maid in the living room, a cook in the kitchen and a whore in the bedroom. I said I'd hire the other two and take care of the bedroom bit.

JERRY HALL   US model and actress.

9 I expect that Woman will be the last thing civilized by Man.

GEORGE MEREDITH (1828–1909) British novelist.

10 One tongue is sufficient for a woman.

JOHN MILTON (1608–74) English poet.
On being asked whether he would allow his daughters to learn foreign languages

11 Scarce, sir. Mighty scarce.

MARK TWAIN (Samuel Langhorne Clemens; 1835–1910)
US writer.
Responding to the question 'In a world without women what
would men become?'

12 Once a woman has given you her heart you can
never get rid of the rest of her.

JOHN VANBRUGH

13 Women have served all these centuries as looking-
glasses possessing the magic and delicious power
of reflecting the figure of man at twice its natural
size.

VIRGINIA WOOLF (1882–1941) British novelist.

WORK

---

1 One cubic foot less of space and it would have constituted adultery.

ROBERT BENCHLEY (1889–1945) US humorist.
Describing an office shared with Dorothy Parker

2 Whatsoever thy hand findeth to do, do it with thy
might; for there is no work, nor device, nor knowledge, nor wisdom, in the grave, whither thou
goest.

BIBLE: ECCLESIASTES

3 Industrial relations are like sexual relations. It's better between two consenting parties.

VIC FEATHER (1908–76) British trade-union leader.

4 By working faithfullyeight hours a day you may eventually get to be a boss and work twelve hours a day.

ROBERT FROST (1875–1963) US poet.

5 The way to get things done is not to mind who gets the credit of doing them.

BENJAMIN JOWETT (1817–93) British theologian.

6 Happy is the man with a wife to tell him what to do and a secretary to do it.

LORD MANCROFT (1917–87) British businessman and writer.

7 Be nice to people on your way up because you'll meet 'em on your way down.

WILSON MIZNER (1876–1933) US writer and wit.
Also attributed to Jimmy Durante

8 They say hard work never hurt anybody, but I figure why take the chance.

RONALD REAGAN (1911–) US Republican president.

9 It might be said that it is the ideal of the employer to have production without employees and the ideal of the employee is to have income without work.

E. F. SCHUMACHER (1911–77) German-born economist.

10 Work is the curse of the drinking classes.

OSCAR WILDE (1854–1900) Irish-born British dramatist.

11 If two men on the same job agree all the time, then one is useless. If they disagree all the time, then both are useless.

DARRYL F. ZANUCK (1902–79) US film producer.

YOUTH

1   Youth is something very new: twenty years ago no one mentioned it.

COCO CHANEL   (1883–1971)   French dress designer.

2   The young always have the same problem – how to rebel and conform at the same time. They have now solved this by defying their parents and copying one another.

QUENTIN CRISP   (?1910–   )   Model, publicist, and writer.

3   Youth will come here and beat on my door, and force its way in.

HENRIK IBSEN   (1828–1906)   Norwegian dramatist.

4   Towering in the confidence of twenty-one.

SAMUEL JOHNSON   (1709–84)   British lexicographer.

5   The atrocious crime of being a young man . . . I shall neither attempt to palliate nor deny.

WILLIAM PITT THE ELDER   (1708–78)   British statesman.

6   My salad days,
When I was green in judgment, cold in blood,
To say as I said then!

WILLIAM SHAKESPEARE   (1564–1616)   English dramatist and critic.

7   Live as long as you may, the first twenty years are the longest half of your life.

ROBERT SOUTHEY   (1774–1843)   British poet.

KEYWORD INDEX

A

abroad an honest man sent to lie
a. for . . . his country
DIPLOMACY, 4

absence A. is to love   LEAVING, 4

accelerator You just press the a.
to the floor and steer left
SPORT, 12

ace someone else was about to
play the a.   CRITICISM, 2

achieved Nothing great was ever
a.   ENTHUSIASM, 1

acquaintance hope our a. may be
a long 'un   SPEECHES, 3

act character actor is one who
cannot a.   OCCUPATIONS, 8

actor a. is something less than a
man   OCCUPATIONS, 2
a. . . . reminds you of an animal
OCCUPATIONS, 9
Every a. in his heart
OCCUPATIONS, 10
great a. . . . lousy husband
OCCUPATIONS, 4
greatest love affairs . . . involved
one a.   OCCUPATIONS, 7
When an a. has money
OCCUPATIONS, 3

actors patience with the jealousies
. . . of a.   OCCUPATIONS, 5
pick out a. by the glazed look
OCCUPATIONS, 11

actress an a. to be a success
OCCUPATIONS, 1
great a. . . . the devil
OCCUPATIONS, 4

actresses A. will happen
OCCUPATIONS, 6

admiring the cure for a. the
House of Lords   HOUSES OF
PARLIAMENT, 2

adolescence maturity is only a
short break in a.   AGE, 8

adores he a. his maker   CONCEIT, 3

adultery commit a. at one end
ADULTERY, 2
the Tasmanians, who never committed a.   ADULTERY, 3
would have constituted a.   WORK, 1

advantage The a. of doing one's
praising   PRAISE, 1

adventure Marriage is the only a.
open to the cowardly
WEDDINGS, 22

advice A. is seldom welcome
ADVICE, 1
intended to give you some a.
ADVICE, 2
woman seldom asks a.   WOMEN, 1
yet to hear . . . earnest a. from my
seniors   ADVICE, 4

against I'm not a. the police
OCCUPATIONS, 81

age A. cannot wither her
COMPLIMENTS, 3
a. finds out was dew   AGE, 3
I prefer old a. to the alternative
AGE, 4

aged a. diplomats . . . bored than
for young men to die
DIPLOMACY, 1

agenda Our a. is now exhausted
AGREEMENT, 2

aging A. . . . the only . . . way to
live a long time   AGE, 1

agree a. to a thing in principle
AGREEMENT, 1
don't say you a. with me
AGREEMENT, 3
If two men on the same job a.
WORK, 11

agreement My people and I have
come to an a.   FREEDOM, 1

ain't bet you a hundred bucks he
a. in here   FUNERALS, 3

airplane The a. stays up because
it doesn't have the time to fall
SCIENCE, 3

aisle A.. Altar. Hymn WEDDINGS, 15

alcohol A. . . . enables Parliament
to do things at eleven
DRINKING, 15
A. is like love   DRINKING, 5

alive not one will still be a. in a
hundred years' time MORTALITY, 7

all a man, take him for a. in a.
COMPLIMENTS, 4

altar Aisle. A.. Hymn WEDDINGS, 15

alternative I prefer old age to the
a. AGE, 4

amateur the last time that I will
take part as an a. FUNERALS, 1

amplified I'm being a. by the
mike SPEECHES, 2

amuse cherish our friends not for
their ability to a. us FRIENDSHIP, 10

ancestors when his half-civilized
a. were hunting the wild boar
JEWS, 1

anecdotage man fell into his a.
AGE, 6

angel In heaven an a. is nobody in
particular EQUALITY, 3

angels A. can fly SERIOUSNESS, 1

animal Man is the only a. . . . on
friendly terms with the victims
. . . he eats HYPOCRISY, 1
This a. is very bad
SELF-PRESERVATION, 1

animals a. . . . know nothing . . .
of what people say about them
ANIMALS, 5
But if we stop loving a. ANIMALS, 4
There are two things for which a.
are . . . envied ANIMALS, 5

another I would have given you
a. CHIVALRY, 2

answer give a. as need requireth
EDUCATION, 1
more than the wisest man can a.
EDUCATION, 4

anybody who you are, you aren't
a. FAME, 3

anyone a. here whom I have not
insulted SPEECHES, 23

apologize a good rule in life
never to a. APOLOGIES, 3

apparatus *Brain*, n. An a. with
which we think EDUCATION, 2

applause I want to thank you for
stopping the a. SPEECHES, 5

appreciation looks back with a.
to the brilliant teachers
OCCUPATIONS, 116

Arabs The Jews and A. should . . .
settle their differences RELIGION, 1

archaeologist An a. is the best
husband WEDDINGS, 9

archbishop the sign of an a. is a
double-cross OCCUPATIONS, 28

arguments A. are to be avoided
ARGUMENTS, 6

aristocracy a. . . . government by
the badly educated DEMOCRACY, 2

arm Don't carry away that a. till I
have . . . my ring PRACTICALITY, 1

arm'd a. with more than complete
steel JUSTICE, 1

army If you don't want to use the
a., I should like to borrow it
SARCASM, 1

arrest My father didn't create you
to a. me OCCUPATIONS, 83

arrow Every a. . . . feels the attraction of earth AMBITION, 2

art Modern a. is what happens
OCCUPATIONS, 12
Mr Goldwyn . . . you are only
interested in a. ART, 6

artist a. must know how to convince OCCUPATIONS, 18
a. who always paints the same
scene pleases the public
OCCUPATIONS, 19
believe only what an a. does
OCCUPATIONS, 14

artists A. . . . they live mainly in
the red OCCUPATIONS, 16

ask To labour and not a. for any
reward SELFLESSNESS, 1

aspect Meet in her a.
COMPLIMENTS, 1

aspirations The young have a.
AGE, 18

ass average schoolmaster is . . .
essentially an a. OCCUPATIONS, 118

attack love until after the first a.
LOVE, 3

attention take his a. away from
the universe PRAYER, 1

attraction Every arrow . . . feels
the a. of earth AMBITION, 2

audience enjoy appearing before a
British a. SPEECHES, 24
the a. was a disaster SPEECHES, 27

Australia guess . . . he was born
in A. PLACES, 18

author a. is a man of genius
OCCUPATIONS, 23
a. who speaks about his own
books OCCUPATIONS, 21
dangerous to an a. as silence
OCCUPATIONS, 24

authority No morality can be
founded on a. MORALITY, 2

teacher should have maximal a.
OCCUPATIONS, 121

B

babies If men had to have b.
CHILDREN, 4

baby Every b. born into the world
CHILDREN, 5

bachelor Never trust . . . a b. too near
WEDDINGS, 18

bachelors reasons for b. to go out
WOMEN, 6

back any of you at the b. who do not hear me
SPEECHES, 1

bad she was a very b. cook
SNOBBERY, 3

when I'm b. I'm better
SEX, 11

bald being b. – one can hear snowflakes
APPEARANCE, 2

ball Casting a b. at three straight sticks
SPORT, 5

bandits Critics! . . . / Those cut-throat b.
OCCUPATIONS, 33

bands Brass b. are all very well in their place
MUSIC, 2

banned any book should be b.
CENSORSHIP, 3

bargains rule for b.
BUSINESS, 2

based All progress is b.
PROGRESS, 2

bat They came to see me b. not to see you bowl!
SPORT, 3

battalions God is always on the side of the big b.
POWER, 6

God is on the side not of the heavy b.
POWER, 7

battle preferred to go into b. sitting down
OCCUPATIONS, 107

bear-baiting Puritan hated b.
MORALITY, 4

beautiful most b. things . . . are the most useless
BEAUTY, 4

beauty A thing of b. is a joy for ever
BEAUTY, 1

b. is only sin deep
BEAUTY, 5

B. is truth, truth b.
BEAUTY, 2

Clad in the b. of a thousand stars
BEAUTY, 3

She walks in b.
COMPLIMENTS, 1

The pain passes, but the b. remains
ENDURANCE, 3

because B. it is there
ACHIEVEMENT, 3

bed Never go to b. mad
ARGUMENTS, 2

bedroom whore in the b.
WOMEN, 8

beg only the poor . . . are forbidden to b.
POVERTY, 1

begin B. low, speak slow
SPEECHES, 7

when the guns b. to shoot
OCCUPATIONS, 103

believe don't b. in . . . true love until after the first attack
LOVE, 3

inclined to b. those whom we do not know
TRUST, 1

it brings you luck whether you b. . . . or not
SUPERSTITION, 1

you must b. in God
FAITH, 2

benefactors gratitude to most b. is the same as . . . for dentists
INGRATITUDE, 1

benevolence husband render unto the wife due b.
WEDDINGS, 6

best all that's b. of dark and bright
COMPLIMENTS, 1

we live in the b. of all possible worlds
OPTIMISM, 1

betraying if I had to choose between b. my country and b. my friend
BETRAYAL, 1

betrothed a bride's attitude towards her b.
WEDDINGS, 15

better b. to marry than to burn
WEDDINGS, 7

when I'm bad I'm b.
SEX, 11

Bibles they have the land and we have the B.
RELIGION, 3

bird-cage a b. played with toasting-forks
MUSIC, 4

Robert Houdin who . . . invented the vanishing b. trick
SPEECHES, 26

birth From b. to age eighteen, a girl needs good parents
AGE, 24

birthday A diplomat . . . always remembers a woman's b.
AGE, 10

bishop blonde to make a b. kick a hole
APPEARANCE, 1

How can a b. marry
OCCUPATIONS, 29

the symbol of a b. is a crook
OCCUPATIONS, 28

blank Where were you fellows

buck The b. stops here
RESPONSIBILITY, 2
bucks bet you a hundred b. he
ain't in here FUNERALS, 3
buds the darling b. of May
COMPLIMENTS, 5
building twenty years of marriage
make her . . . like a public b.
MARRIAGE, 10
bull Better send them a Papal B.
MISTAKES, 1
When you take the b. by the
horns CHANCE, 1
burn better to marry than to b.
WEDDINGS, 7
burned Whenever books are b.
CENSORSHIP, 1
burning To keep a lamp b.
CHARITY, 3
business b. sagacity reduces itself
BUSINESS, 11
B. underlies everything in our national life BUSINESS, 13
bust It's a funny thing about that
b. AGE, 21
butter b. wouldn't melt in her
mouth INSULTS, 3
butterfly Happiness is like a b.
HAPPINESS, 2

C

Caesar C.'s wife PURITY, 2
calamities C. are of two kinds
MISFORTUNE, 1
calf but the c. won't get much
sleep MISTRUST, 1
cancel to c. half a Line DESTINY, 1
candle little c. throws his beams
GOOD, 4
candles She would rather light c.
than curse the darkness
COMPLIMENTS, 7
cards sorry I have not learned to
play at c. GAMES, 5
wonderful to see persons of the
best sense . . . shuffling and dividing a pack of c. GAMES, 1
catastrophe When a man confronts
c. . . . a woman looks in her mirror
MEN AND WOMEN, 9
Catherine I'm glad you like my C.
SEX, 9
celebrity A c. . . . works hard . . .
to become known FAME, 1

celery Genuineness . . . Like c.
SINCERITY, 2
censorship C. . . . depraving and
corrupting CENSORSHIP, 2
chaff An editor . . . separates the
wheat from the c.
OCCUPATIONS, 53
champagne like a glass of c. that
has stood HOUSES OF PARLIAMENT, 1
water flowed like c. ABSTINENCE, 3
Charing-Cross the full tide of
human existence is at C.
LONDON, 1
Chartreuse religious system that
produced green C. DRINKING, 13
chastity Give me c. and continence MORALITY, 1
cheating Peace . . . a period of c.
PEACE, 1
chess Life's too short for c.
GAMES, 2
victim of c. GAMES, 3
child c. of five would understand
this SIMPLICITY, 1
What is the use of a new-born c.
TECHNOLOGY, 1
wise father that knows his own c.
FAMILY, 7
childbirth Death and taxes and c.
CHILDREN, 9
children C. have never been very
good at listening CHILDREN, 1
He that has no c. CHILDREN, 11
Never have c. CHILDREN, 14
Parents . . . a disappointment to their
c. CHILDREN, 6
Parents learn a lot from their c.
CHILDREN, 13
Chopin to bridge the awful gap
between Dorothy and C. MUSIC, 1
Christianity C. . . . but why journalism OCCUPATIONS, 57
decay of C. DRINKING, 13
Christians settle their differences
like good C. RELIGION, 1
circumcised When they c. Herbert Samuel INSULTS, 2
circuses bread and c. PUBLIC, 6
city It is a c. where you can see a
sparrow fall IRELAND, 5
civilized c. man cannot live without cooks OCCUPATIONS, 30
Woman will be the last thing c. by
Man WOMEN, 9

clean hard to be funny when you have to be c. HUMOUR, 3

clear His right was c., his will was strong RIGHT, 1
if he could make *me* understand . . . it would be c. to all UNDERSTANDING, 1

clenched You cannot shake hands with a c. fist COMPROMISE, 1

climb Fain would I c., yet fear I to fall AMBITION, 3

climbing c. is performed in the same position with creeping AMBITION, 4

clock colleagues generally present him with a c. LEAVING, 13

clocks hands of c. in railway stations CHILDREN, 3
pass my declining years saluting . . . grandfather c. AGE, 13

close-up Life is a tragedy . . . in c. LIFE, 2

clothes After that you just take the girl's c. off DRINKING, 5
bought her wedding c. WOMEN, 1
pay more for my c. CLOTHES, 1
taking off all her c. CLOTHES, 4

club I don't want to belong to any c. HUMOUR, 6
takes you so far from the c. house SPORT, 7

cock waiting for the c. to crow BETRAYAL, 3

cold she should catch a c. on overexposure TRUTH, 3
threat of a neglected c. is for doctors OCCUPATIONS, 40

comedy Life is . . . a c. in long-shot LIFE, 2

command people c. rather badly LEADERSHIP, 1

commerce honour sinks where c. long prevails BUSINESS, 5

committee A c. is a cul-de-sac BUREAUCRACY, 3
The number one book of the ages was written by a c. BUREAUCRACY, 4

common C. sense is the collection of prejudices PREJUDICE, 1

common-looking The Lord prefers c. people APPEARANCE, 5

Communism C. is like prohibition COMMUNISM, 1

community journalism. . . . keeps us in touch with the ignorance of the c. OCCUPATIONS, 64
Marriage . . . a c. . . . making in all two MARRIAGE, 1

companions c. for middle age WEDDINGS, 3

company never expected justice from a c. BUSINESS, 10

compare c. thee to a summer's day COMPLIMENTS, 5

complaint I want to register a c. COMPLAINTS, 1

concealing Good breeding consists in c. how . . . we think of ourselves MANNERS, 2

condition fools decoyed into our c. WEDDINGS, 16
the Jews have made a contribution to the human c. JEWS, 2

confess Men will c. HUMOUR, 2
only c. our little faults IMPERFECTION, 2

confidence c. of twenty-one YOUTH, 4

conform how to rebel and c. at the same time YOUTH, 2

conscience freedom of speech, freedom of c., and the prudence never to practise . . . them FREEDOM, 7

consent No one can make you feel inferior without your c. INFERIORITY, 1

constant A c. guest HOSPITALITY, 2

continence Give me chastity and c. MORALITY, 1
that melancholy sexual perversion known as c. ABSTINENCE, 5

Continent On the C. people have good food MANNERS, 1

Continental C. people have sex life PLACES, 15

contraception a terrific story about oral c. CONTRACEPTION, 1

contraceptives C. should be used CONTRACEPTION, 2

contradicts One often c. an opinion ARGUMENTS, 3

conversation make his c. perfectly delightful SPEECH, 15

Your ignorance cramps my c.
IGNORANCE, 1
conversationalist the c. who
adds 'in other words' SPEECH, 12
cook c. was a good c.
OCCUPATIONS, 32
good thing about him is his c.
OCCUPATIONS, 31
she was a very bad c. SNOBBERY, 3
cooks civilized man cannot live
without c. OCCUPATIONS, 30
copying by defying their parents
and c. one another YOUTH, 2
corrupt Power tends to c.
POWER, 1
cost To give and not to count the
c. SELFLESSNESS, 1
count If you can . . . c. your
money you are not . . . rich man
MONEY, 4
country an honest man sent to lie
abroad for . . . his c. DIPLOMACY, 4
our c., right or wrong
PATRIOTISM, 1
The past is a foreign c. PAST, 3
understanding the problems of
running a c. OCCUPATIONS, 88
couple A married c. are well
suited MARRIAGE, 5
courage good deal of physical c.
to ride a horse ANIMALS, 2
courting When you are c. a nice
girl SCIENCE, 2
cowardly Marriage is the only adventure open to the c.
WEDDINGS, 22
cows daring . . . to explain . . . that
c. can be eaten RELIGION, 2
cradle Between the c. and the
grave MORTALITY, 3
create My father didn't c. you to
arrest me OCCUPATIONS, 83
Creation Had I been present at
the C. UNIVERSE, 1
credit The way to get things done
is not to mind who gets the c.
WORK, 5
creditors my oldest c. would
hardly know me APPEARANCE, 3
creeds So many gods, so many c.
KINDNESS, 2
creeping climbing is performed in
the same position with c.
AMBITION, 4

cricket c. as organised loafing
SPORT, 10
crime The atrocious c. of being a
young man YOUTH, 5
critic A c. is a man who
OCCUPATIONS, 38
c. is a legless man OCCUPATIONS, 37
drama c. is a person who surprises the playwright
OCCUPATIONS, 36
ever seen a dramatic c. in the
daytime OCCUPATIONS, 39
critics Asking a working writer
. . . about c. OCCUPATIONS, 35
C.! . . . Those cut-throat bandits
OCCUPATIONS, 33
heaves in the presence of c.
OCCUPATIONS, 34
crook the symbol of a bishop is a
c. OCCUPATIONS, 28
cross no c., no crown
ENDURANCE, 2
crossword an optimist . . . fills up
his c. puzzle in ink OPTIMISM, 2
crow waiting for the cock to c.
BETRAYAL, 3
crowd a c. like that . . . brings a
lump to my wallet MONEY, 14
flock of sheep . . . make a c. of men
PUBLIC, 1
crown no cross, no c.
ENDURANCE, 2
cubic One c. foot less WORK, 1
cul-de-sac A committee is a c.
BUREAUCRACY, 3
cure the c. for admiring the House
of Lords HOUSES OF PARLIAMENT, 2
curse She would rather light candles than c. the darkness
COMPLIMENTS, 7
Work is the c. of the drinking
classes WORK, 10
curtain I saw it at a disadvantage
– the c. was up CRITICISM, 12
cushion Like a c., he always bore
INSULTS, 1
custom A c. loathsome to the
eye, hateful to the nose
SMOKING, 3
c. stale Her infinite variety
COMPLIMENTS, 3
customers When you are skinning
your c. BUSINESS, 6

D

dancers a perfectly ghastly season it's been for you Spanish d. CHARITY, 1

dark Genuineness only thrives in the d. SINCERITY, 2

darkness She would rather light candles than curse the d. COMPLIMENTS, 7

dates Its history d. from today ROYALTY, 2

day compare thee to a summer's d. COMPLIMENTS, 5
I look upon every d. to be lost FRIENDSHIP, 5
thou knowest not what a d. may bring forth FUTURE, 1

days d. of wine and roses MORTALITY, 1

dead But he's just as d. as if he'd been wrong RIGHT, 1
He was a great patriot . . . provided . . . that he really is d. COMPLIMENTS, 9
I've just read that I am d. OBITUARIES, 2
The past is the only d. thing PAST, 5

dear D. 338171 HUMOUR, 5

death d. after life does greatly please DEATH, 8
D. and taxes and childbirth CHILDREN, 9
d. . . . the least of all evils DEATH, 3
Football isn't a matter of life and d. SPORT, 9
Reports of my d. are greatly exaggerated OBITUARIES, 3
the d. of Little Nell without laughing INSENSITIVITY, 1
what a man still plans at the end shows the . . . injustice in his d. DEATH, 4

debt A promise made is a d. unpaid PROMISES, 2

declining pass my d. years saluting . . . grandfather clocks AGE, 13

decompose d. in a barrel of porter FUNERALS, 4

decrepit you are not yet d. enough AGE, 6

deed good d. in a naughty world GOOD, 4

deep beauty is only sin d. BEAUTY, 5

defend I disapprove of what you say, but I will d. . . . your right to say it FREEDOM, 8

defying by d. their parents and copying one another YOUTH, 1

delightful make his conversation perfectly d. SPEECH, 15

democracy D. . . . government by the uneducated DEMOCRACY, 2
D. means government by discussion DEMOCRACY, 1
not the voting that's d. DEMOCRACY, 3

dentists gratitude to most benefactors is the same as . . . for d. INGRATITUDE, 1

depression Recession . . . a neighbour loses . . . d. . . . you lose ECONOMICS, 1

deserve I have arthritis, and I don't d. that either AWARDS, 1

deserves At 50, everyone has the face he d. AGE, 14

desire a universal innate d. PROGRESS, 2
d. to be praised twice over PRAISE, 2
It provokes the d. DRINKING, 14

despise some other Englishman d. him PLACES, 17

destination I do not think this poem will reach its d. CRITICISM, 10

destroys d. one of the works of God we call him a sportsman HUNTING, 3

devil the D. knows Latin CHILDREN, 8
the world, the flesh, and the d. OCCUPATIONS, 62

diamonds My goodness those d. are lovely GOOD, 6
to give him d. back MEN, 3

dictation God wrote it. I merely did his d. ACHIEVEMENT, 6

die argue that I shall some day d. OCCUPATIONS, 79
If a man hasn't discovered something that he would d. for IDEALISM, 1

dies It matters not how a man d.
DEATH, 5
differences d. in taste or opinion
are irritating ARGUMENTS, 1
The Jews and Arabs should . . .
settle their d. RELIGION, 1
difficult D. do you call it, Sir
CRITICISM, 5
It is d. to be humble HUMILITY, 1
only the first step that is d.
BEGINNING, 1
dined when Thomas Jefferson d.
alone SPEECHES, 4
diplomat A d. . . . always remembers a woman's birthday AGE, 10
diplomats aged d. to be bored
DIPLOMACY, 1
disapprove I d. of what you say,
but I will defend . . . your right
to say it FREEDOM, 8
disaster the audience was a d.
SPEECHES, 27
disease Evil comes . . . like the
d.; good . . . like the doctor
GOOD, 1
diseases Doctors . . . cure d. of
which they know less
OCCUPATIONS, 49
disgrace a d. to our family name
of Wagstaff FAMILY, 4
dismal situation so d. that a
policeman OCCUPATIONS, 80
dissipated still keep looking so d.
DEBAUCHERY, 1
distance The d. doesn't matter
BEGINNING, 1
do I am to d. what I please
FREEDOM, 1
doctor A young d. makes a
humpy graveyard OCCUPATIONS, 46
d. found . . . last disorder mortal
OCCUPATIONS, 42
d. takes the fee OCCUPATIONS, 41
Evil comes . . . like the disease;
good . . . like the d. GOOD, 1
He has been a d. a year now
OCCUPATIONS, 48
doctors D. . . . prescribe
medicines of which they know
little OCCUPATIONS, 49
D. think a lot of patients are
cured OCCUPATIONS, 43
D. will have more lives to answer
for OCCUPATIONS, 45

threat of a neglected cold is for d.
OCCUPATIONS, 40
dog A door is what a d. is . . . on
the wrong side of DOGS, 2
The great pleasure of a d. DOGS, 1
dogs I loathe people who keep d.
DOGS, 3
like asking a lamp-post . . . about
d. OCCUPATIONS, 35
dollars What's a thousand d.
MONEY, 7
done The way to get things d. is
not to mind who gets the credit
WORK, 5
don't-knows One day the d. will
get in GOVERNMENT, 1
door A d. is what a dog is . . . on
the wrong side of DOGS, 2
Youth will come . . . beat on my
d. YOUTH, 3
down I started at the top and
worked my way d.
ACHIEVEMENT, 7
dreamt I d. that I was making a
speech SPEECHES, 14
dreary Dying is a very dull, d. affair DEATH, 7
drink d. may be said to be an
equivocator with lechery
DRINKING, 14
no one has yet found a way to d.
for a living DRINKING, 10
One reason I don't d. DRINKING, 2
There are five reasons we should
d. DRINKING, 1
drinkers no verse can give pleasure . . . that is written by d. of
water DRINKING, 6
drinking D. is the soldier's pleasure OCCUPATIONS, 100
resolve to give up smoking, d.
and loving ABSTINENCE, 4
smoking cigars and . . . d. of alcohol before, after, and if need be
during all meals SMOKING, 2
Work is the curse of the d.
classes WORK, 10
driver in the d.'s seat POWER, 2
drug Words are . . . the most powerful d. SPEECH, 11
Dublin D., though . . . much worse
than London PLACES, 11
duty a stupid man . . . always declares that it is his d. EXCUSES, 3

What's a man's first d. SINCERITY, 3
dying D. is a very dull, dreary affair DEATH, 7
'Tis not the d. for a faith FAITH, 3
dykes our d. . . . are ten feet
deep BOASTS, 8

E

ears device to keep the e. from
grating EDUCATION, 5
earth mine were princes of the e.
JEWS, 1
The meek do not inherit the e.
HUMILITY, 2
eat E. as much as you like
OBESITY, 3
eaten daring . . . to explain . . .
that cows can be e. RELIGION, 2
eating E.'s going to be a whole
new ball game LEAVING, 10
eats Man is the only animal . . . on
friendly terms with the victims
. . . he e. HYPOCRISY, 1
economist Give me a one-handed
e. ECONOMICS, 3
economists All races have . . . e.,
with the exception of the Irish
IRELAND, 1
If all e. were laid end to end
ECONOMICS, 2
editor An e. . . . separates the
wheat from the chaff
OCCUPATIONS, 53
e. should have a pimp for a
brother OCCUPATIONS, 51
newspaper e. and . . . a fellow
with a tapeworm OCCUPATIONS, 52
education E. is an admirable
thing EDUCATION, 13
E. is . . . the soul of a society
EDUCATION, 3
schooling interfere with my e.
EDUCATION, 11
When a man's e. is finished
EDUCATION, 6
egalitarianism The majestic e. of
the law EQUALITY, 1
egotist E., n. A person . . . more
interested in himself CONCEIT, 2
Egyptians the E. worshipped an
insect OCCUPATIONS, 84
eighteen From birth to age e., a
girl needs good parents AGE, 24

she speaks e. languages. And she
can't say 'No' in any of them
SEX, 8
elders miss not the discourse of
the e. EDUCATION, 1
elopement an e. would be preferable WEDDINGS, 1
eloquence Talking and e. are not
the same SPEECH, 10
else Suppose it had been someone
e. who found you like this
ADULTERY, 4
embalmer A triumph of the e.'s
art INSULTS, 4
employed innocently e. than in
getting money MONEY, 5
employer ideal of the e. . . . production without employees
WORK, 9
employers e. wanting all sorts of
servants OCCUPATIONS, 96
employment I will undoubtedly
have to seek . . . gainful e.
LEAVING, 1
empty You can't think rationally
on an e. stomach THINKING, 2
end of making many books there
is no e. BOOKS, 1
Yes, to the very e. ENDURANCE, 4
enemies do not have to forgive my
e. RUTHLESSNESS, 2
Even a paranoid can have e.
ENEMIES, 1
enemy hasn't an e. in the world
POPULARITY, 2
It takes your e. and your friend
. . . to hurt you ENEMIES, 2
we must be just to our e.
OCCUPATIONS, 27
England E. is a paradise for
women PLACES, 3
E. . . . the envy of less happy
lands PLACES, 8
in E. people have good table manners MANNERS, 1
English The baby doesn't under-
stand E. CHILDREN, 8
the E. have hot-water bottles
PLACES, 15
The E. have no respect for their
language PLACES, 17
The E. may not like music
MUSIC, 3
Englishman Am I not punished

enough in not being born an E. PLACES, 20

An E. . . . forms an orderly queue of one PLACES, 14

never find an E. among the underdogs PLACES, 21

Remember that you are an E. PLACES, 16

some other E. despise him PLACES, 17

Englishmen to create Frenchmen in the image of E. PLACES, 5

enigma a riddle wrapped in a mystery inside an e. PLACES, 7

enjoy Certainly, there is nothing else here to e. PARTIES, 3

enough It comes soon e. FUTURE, 3

enthusiasm Nothing great was ever achieved without e. ENTHUSIASM, 1

We were as nearly bored as e. would permit CRITICISM, 4

enthusiastic Latins are tenderly e. PLACES, 9

envied There are two things for which animals are . . . e. ANIMALS, 5

envy 2 percent moral, 48 percent indignation and 50 percent e. MORALITY, 8

equal Everybody should have an e. chance EQUALITY, 4

equally I hate everyone e. HATE, 1

equipping e. us with a neck COURAGE, 2

eternity over the Bridge of Sighs into e. DEATH, 6

evening thou art fairer than the e. air BEAUTY, 3

everyone I hate e. equally HATE, 1

evidence Most men . . . give e. against their own understanding SPEECH, 7

evil E. comes . . . like the disease; good . . . like the doctor GOOD, 1

evils animals . . . know nothing of future e. ANIMALS, 5

death . . . the least of all e. DEATH, 3

Whenever I'm caught between two e. VICE, 1

exaggerated Reports of my death are greatly e. OBITUARIES, 3

excess Nothing succeeds like e. EXCESS, 2

excluded when you have e. the impossible TRUTH, 4

executive salary of the chief e. . . . not a market award for achievement BUSINESS, 4

exercise E. is bunk SPORT, 2

exhausted Our agenda is now e. AGREEMENT, 2

experience The triumph of hope over e. WEDDINGS, 13

expert An e. . . . has made all the mistakes . . . in a very narrow field EXPERTS, 1

ex-president No candidate . . . elected e. by such a large majority FAILURE, 3

extinct the Tasmanians . . . are now e. ADULTERY, 3

extraordinary the most e. collection of talent SPEECHES, 4

eye A custom loathsome to the e., hateful to the nose SMOKING, 3

less in this than meets the e. CRITICISM, 1

man who looks you . . . in the e. . . . hiding something INSINCERITY, 1

eyes Your e. shine like the pants COMPLIMENTS, 2

F

face At 50, everyone has the f. he deserves AGE, 14

I never forget a f., but I'll make an exception MEMORY, 1

facts f. must never get in the way of truth OCCUPATIONS, 58

fail Others must f. RUTHLESSNESS, 3

fairer thou art f. than the evening air BEAUTY, 3

faith no need for any other f. than . . . f. in human beings FAITH, 1

'Tis not the dying for a f. FAITH, 3

fall Fain would I climb, yet fear I to f. AMBITION, 3

The airplane stays up because it doesn't have the time to f. SCIENCE, 3

false beware of f. prophets DECEPTION, 1

fame blush to find it f. GOOD, 3

The book written against f. . . . has the author's name on the title-page HYPOCRISY, 2

family f. always creeps back FAMILY, 5

farce Parliament is the longest running f. GOVERNMENT, 2

farewells f. should be sudden LEAVING, 5

farmer good f. is . . . a handy man OCCUPATIONS, 55

farmers f., flourish and complain OCCUPATIONS, 54

fascinates I like work; it f. me IDLENESS, 2

fat Outside every f. man . . . an even fatter man OBESITY, 1
there's a thin man inside every f. man OBESITY, 2

fate when F. summons MORTALITY, 2

father a wise f. that knows his own child FAMILY, 7
My f. didn't create you to arrest me OCCUPATIONS, 83
No man is responsible for his f. FAMILY, 8

fattening the things I really like . . . are either immoral, illegal, or f. PLEASURE, 2

fault only one f.. It was . . . lousy CRITICISM, 9

faults f., do not fear to abandon them IMPERFECTION, 1
only confess our little f. IMPERFECTION, 2

favour accepts a smaller as a f. INJUSTICE, 1

fear only thing we have to f. is f. itself COURAGE, 3

feast Paris is a moveable f. PLACES, 10

fee doctor takes the f. OCCUPATIONS, 41

feeding Spoon f. . . . teaches us nothing but the shape of the spoon EDUCATION, 7

feet Alan will always land on somebody's f. HUMOUR, 7
both f. firmly planted in the air IDEALISM, 3

fence The . . . gentleman has sat so long on the f. NONCOMMITMENT, 2

50 At 5., everyone has the face he deserves AGE, 14

fifty You'll see, when you're f. AGE, 19

fight easier to f. for one's principles PRINCIPLES, 1
To f. and not to heed the wounds SELFLESSNESS, 1
You cannot f. against the future PROGRESS, 5

finer every baby . . . is a f. one CHILDREN, 5

finger Moving F. writes DESTINY, 1

fire what wind is to f. LEAVING, 4

fires Husbands are like f. WEDDINGS, 11

first Because of my title, I was the f. COURAGE, 1

fist You cannot shake hands with a clenched f. COMPROMISE, 1

five child of f. would understand this practise f. things SIMPLICITY, 1
practise f. things VIRTUE, 1

flesh the world, the f., and the devil OCCUPATIONS, 62

flowed water f. like champagne ABSTINENCE, 3

fly A f., Sir, may sting a stately horse CRITICISM, 6

foe he is the sworn f. of our nation OCCUPATIONS, 27

Folies-Bergère A psychiatrist is a man who goes to the F. OCCUPATIONS, 95

folk-dancing except incest and f. EXPERIENCE, 1

follies The f. which a man regrets REGRET, 2

follow I have to f. them, I am their leader LEADERSHIP, 2

food On the Continent people have good f. MANNERS, 1

fool the greatest f. may ask more EDUCATION, 4
You can f. too many of the people DECEPTION, 3

foolish anything very f. PRINCIPLES, 3

fools f. decoyed into our condition WEDDINGS, 16

football F. isn't a matter of life and death SPORT, 9

foreign pronounce f. names as he chooses PRONUNCIATION, 1

forget Painter . . . has first to f. all the roses   OCCUPATIONS, 15
Were it not better to f.   REGRET, 1

forgive do not have to f. my enemies   RUTHLESSNESS, 2

formidable Examinations are f.   EDUCATION, 4

fortune to make your f. . . . let people see . . . it is in their interests to promote yours   SUCCESS, 2

forty-five That should assure us of . . . f. minutes of undisturbed privacy   INATTENTION, 1

found Suppose it had been someone else who f. you like this   ADULTERY, 4

fox The f. knows many things   KNOWLEDGE, 1

frames The finest collection of f.   ART, 5

free the truth shall make you f.   TRUTH, 2
truth that makes men f.   TRUTH, 1
We have to believe in f. will   FREEDOM, 6

freedom F. is the right to tell . . . do not want to hear   FREEDOM, 5
f. of speech, f. of conscience, and the prudence never to practise . . . them   FREEDOM, 7
Until you've lost your reputation, you never realize . . . what f. really is   REPUTATION, 2

Frenchmen to create F. in the image of Englishmen   PLACES, 5

Freud The trouble with F.   OCCUPATIONS, 93

friend a new f. is as new wine   FRIENDSHIP, 1
forsake not an old f.   FRIENDSHIP, 1
good f. that she will throw   FRIENDSHIP, 9
It takes your enemy and your f. . . . to hurt you   ENEMIES, 2
no man is useless while he has a f.   FRIENDSHIP, 8

friendly Man is the only animal . . . on f. terms with the victims . . . he eats   HYPOCRISY, 1

friends cherish our f. not for their ability to amuse us   FRIENDSHIP, 10
Money can't buy f.   MONEY, 8

none of his f. like him   POPULARITY, 2
treat your f. a little better   FRIENDSHIP, 4
you choose your f.   FAMILY, 3

friendship f. closes its eyes   FRIENDSHIP, 7
Men seem to kick f. around like a football   FRIENDSHIP, 6

frighten by God, they f. me   OCCUPATIONS, 108

fruit Ignorance is like a delicate exotic f.   IGNORANCE, 3

fun the most f. I ever had without laughing   SEX, 2

funerals If you don't go to other men's f.   FUNERALS, 2

funny hard to be f. when you have to be clean   HUMOUR, 3

future I have seen the f.   FUTURE, 4
I never think of the f.   FUTURE, 3
people who live in the f.   PROGRESS, 1
The f. is made of the same stuff   FUTURE, 5
You cannot fight against the f.   PROGRESS, 5

G

gaiety the only concession to g.   PLACES, 19

gained learning hath g. most   BOOKS, 3

gainful I will undoubtedly have to seek . . . g. employment   LEAVING, 1

gains no g. without pains   SUCCESS, 5

game It's more than a g.. It's an institution   SPORT, 4
man's idea in a card g. is war   GAMES, 4

Garbo one sees in G. sober   COMPLIMENTS, 8

gatekeeper After I die, I shall return to earth as a g. of a bordello   MUSIC, 8

gather G. ye rosebuds while ye may   PRESENT, 1

generalizations All g. are dangerous   GENERALIZATIONS, 1

generation Each g. imagines itself . . . more intelligent   AGE, 15

genius a country full of g., but

with absolutely no talent IRELAND, 4

A g.! For thirty-seven years I've practiced . . . and now they call me a g. ACHIEVEMENT, 5

G. is one per cent inspiration ACHIEVEMENT, 2

Nothing, except my g. BOASTS, 6

gentleman A g. . . . wouldn't hit a woman with his hat on CHIVALRY, 1

genuineness G. only thrives in the dark SINCERITY, 2

geographical India is a g. term PLACES, 6

George Lloyd G. POWER, 2

giants it is by standing on the shoulders of g. PROGRESS, 6

gift True love's the g. which God has given To man alone LOVE, 6

worth more than the g. GIFTS, 1

girl From birth to age eighteen, a g. needs good parents AGE, 24

Many a man has fallen in love with a g. LOVE, 2

one can . . . see in a little g. the threat of a woman CHILDREN, 6

girls Where . . . boys plan for what . . . young g. plan for whom MEN AND WOMEN, 3

give To g. and not to count the cost SELFLESSNESS, 1

given I would have g. you another CHIVALRY, 2

giving The manner of g. GIFTS, 1

Glasgow never played the G. Empire OCCUPATIONS, 93

glory paths of g. lead but to the grave MORTALITY, 5

go I shall be the last to g. out COURAGE, 1

God Even G. cannot change the past PAST, 2

G. is always on the side of the big battalions POWER, 6

G. is on the side . . . of the best shots POWER, 7

I did not write it. G. wrote it ACHIEVEMENT, 6

you must believe in G. FAITH, 2

gods So many g., so many creeds KINDNESS, 2

godsend good servant is a real g. OCCUPATIONS, 98

golden perhaps, the g. rule ABSTINENCE, 6

Goldwyn Mr G. . . . you are only interested in art ART, 6

golf G. . . . a form of moral effort SPORT, 6

G. is a game whose aim SPORT, 1

G. is a good walk spoiled SPORT, 11

impossible to remember how tragic . . . playing g. SPORT, 8

good Do g. by stealth GOOD, 3

Evil comes . . . like the disease; g. . . . like the doctor GOOD, 1

G. isn't the word CRITICISM, 3

Nothing can harm a g. man GOOD, 5

Whenever two g. people argue over principles PRINCIPLES, 2

When I'm g. I'm very g. SEX, 11

goodbyes never any good dwelling on g. LEAVING, 3

goodness My g. those diamonds are lovely GOOD, 6

gossips No one g. about . . . secret virtues GOSSIP, 1

government a g. organization could do it that quickly BUREAUCRACY, 2

gradually Boys do not grow up g. CHILDREN, 3

grandfather pass my declining years saluting . . . g. clocks AGE, 13

grandmother I murdered my g. this morning INATTENTION, 2

grasp man's reach should exceed his g. AMBITION, 1

grasped journalism what will be g. at once OCCUPATIONS, 60

grave Between the cradle and the g. MORTALITY, 3

no work, nor device, nor knowledge . . . in the g. WORK, 2

paths of glory lead but to the g. MORTALITY, 5

great All my shows are g. BOASTS, 3

you . . . who have made me too g. for my house HOME, 1

green I was g. in judgment YOUTH, 6

religious system that produced g. Chartreuse DRINKING, 13

grief calms one's g. by recounting it SORROW, 1

in much wisdom is much g. WISDOM, 1

Should be past g. REGRET, 3

what's past help /should be past g. REGRET, 3

growing G. old is like being increasingly penalized AGE, 16

grows Nothing g. well in the shade EXCUSES, 1

gun muzzle of my g. as their safest position HUNTING, 5

guns But it's 'Saviour of 'is country' when the g. OCCUPATIONS, 103

H

had you h. it in you CHILDREN, 10

half longest h. of your life YOUTH, 7

One h. . . . cannot understand . . . the other PLEASURE, 1

hands don't raise your h. because I am also nearsighted SPEECHES, 1

To be played with both h. in the pocket MUSIC, 7

You cannot shake h. with a clenched fist COMPROMISE, 1

hanged if they were going to see me h. PUBLIC, 3

happens I just don't want to be there when it h. DEATH, 1

happiness H. is an imaginary condition HAPPINESS, 3

H. is like a butterfly HAPPINESS, 2

H. is no laughing matter HAPPINESS, 4

I thought that success spelled h. HAPPINESS, 2

nothing . . . by which so much h. is produced as by a good tavern DRINKING, 9

happy Ask . . . whether you are h. HAPPINESS, 1

Puritanism – The haunting fear that someone . . . may be h. MORALITY, 5

hardships we shall be glad to remember even these h. ENDURANCE, 6

harpsichord The sound of the h. MUSIC, 4

hat A gentleman . . . wouldn't hit a woman with his h. on CHIVALRY, 1

hate I h. everyone equally HATE, 1

hated I never h. a man enough MEN, 3

hates Everybody h. me POPULARITY, 1

head If you can keep your h. SELF-CONTROL, 2

headmasters H. have powers OCCUPATIONS, 114

hear any of you at the back who do not h. me SPEECHES, 1

truth which men prefer not to h. TRUTH, 1

heart I love thee for a h. that's kind KINDNESS, 1

Once a woman has given you her h. WOMEN, 12

What comes from the h. SINCERITY, 1

heaven H. has granted me no offspring BOASTS, 5

In h. an angel is nobody in particular EQUALITY, 3

what's a h. for AMBITION, 1

heed To fight and not to h. the wounds SELFLESSNESS, 1

hell Italy . . . h. for women PLACES, 3

help the h. of too many physicians MEDICINE, 1

here bet you a hundred bucks he ain't in h. FUNERALS, 3

hiding man who looks you . . . in the eye . . . h. something INSINCERITY, 1

highbrow What is a h. INTELLECT, 5

himself ever written out of reputation but by h. REPUTATION, 1

hire lawyers . . . let out their brains for h. OCCUPATIONS, 70

history Its h. dates from today ROYALTY, 2

lawyer without h. or literature is a mechanic OCCUPATIONS, 78

hit If you would h. the mark AMBITION, 2

holder office sanctifies the h. POWER, 1

home English should give Ireland h. rule IRELAND, 6

H. art gone and ta'en thy wages LEAVING, 11

H. . . . where . . . they have to take you in HOME, 2

I can get all that at h.   THEATRE, 1
honest an h. man sent to lie
  abroad for . . . his country
                      DIPLOMACY, 4
Behold a lawyer, an h. man
                      OCCUPATIONS, 72
honour we're fighting for this
  woman's h.   HONOUR, 1
hope The triumph of h. over experience   WEDDINGS, 13
horns When you take the bull by
  the h. . . .   CHANCE, 1
horse A fly, Sir, may sting a
  stately h.   CRITICISM, 6
good deal of physical courage to
  ride a h.   ANIMALS, 2
I feel as a h. must feel INJUSTICE, 2
I know two things about the h.
                      ANIMALS, 1
To confess that you are totally Ignorant about the H.   ANIMALS, 3
horses England . . . hell for h.
                      PLACES, 3
hospital h. is the assumption on
  the part of the staff   MEDICINE, 2
host of all this h. of men not one
  will still be alive in a hundred
  years' time   MORTALITY, 7
hot-water the English have h.
  bottles   PLACES, 15
Houdin Robert H. who . . . invented the vanishing bird-cage
  trick   SPEECHES, 26
Houdini Harry H.   FUNERALS, 3
hour at the rate of sixty minutes
  an h.   TIME, 1
house A man in the h. is worth two
                      MEN, 5
you, . . . who have made me too
  great for my h.   HOME, 1
House of Commons leader of
  the H.   OCCUPATIONS, 84
House of Lords The H. . . . how
  to care for the elderly   HOUSES OF
                      PARLIAMENT, 3
The H. . . . kept efficient by . . .
  persistent absenteeism HOUSES OF
                      PARLIAMENT, 4
human All that is h. must retrograde   PROGRESS, 4
no need for any other faith than
  . . . faith in h. beings   FAITH, 1
the full tide of h. existence is at
  Charing-Cross   LONDON, 1

humble It is difficult to be h.
                      HUMILITY, 1
humour own up to a lack of h.
                      HUMOUR, 2
hundred bet you a h. bucks he
  ain't in here   FUNERALS, 3
of all this host of men not one will
  still be alive in a h. years' time
                      MORTALITY, 7
hungry she makes h. Where most
  she satisfies   COMPLIMENTS, 3
hunting passion for *h. something*
                      HUNTING, 1
strange . . . to call h. one of them
                      HUNTING, 2
when his half-civilized ancestors
  were h. the wild boar   JEWS, 1
hurry So who's in a h.   DRINKING, 3
hurt it h. too much to laugh
                      FAILURE, 2
It takes your enemy and your
  friend . . . to h. you   ENEMIES, 2
husband An archaeologist is the
  best h.   WEDDINGS, 9
easier to be a lover than a h.
                      WEDDINGS, 5
great actor . . . lousy h.
                      OCCUPATIONS, 4
h. render unto the wife due benevolence   WEDDINGS, 6
Never trust a h. too far
                      WEDDINGS, 18
The h. frae the wife despises
                      WEDDINGS, 8
husbands h. and wives . . . belong
  to different sexes   MEN AND
                      WOMEN, 1
H. are like fires   WEDDINGS, 11
h. to stay at home   WOMEN, 6
hymn Aisle. Altar. H. WEDDINGS, 15

I

ice skating over thin i.   HASTE, 1
idea constant repetition . . . in im-
  printing an i.   PUBLIC, 5
I think it would be a good i.
                      CIVILIZATION, 2
no stand can be made against invasion by an i.   IDEAS, 2
idealist An i. . . . , on noticing that
  a rose smells better than a cabbage   IDEALISM, 2
ideas down which i. are lured and
  . . . strangled   BUREAUCRACY, 3

i. are of more importance than values INTELLECT, 2

idiots most schoolmasters are i. OCCUPATIONS, 120

idleness I. . . . the refuge of weak minds IDLENESS, 1
round of strenuous i. SPORT, 14

if I. you can keep your head SELF-CONTROL, 2

ignorance I. is like a delicate exotic fruit IGNORANCE, 3
journalism. . . . keeps us in touch with the i. of the community OCCUPATIONS, 64
Your i. cramps my conversation IGNORANCE, 1

ignorant To confess that you are totally I. about the Horse ANIMALS, 3

illegal the things I really like . . . are either immoral, i., or fattening PLEASURE, 2

imaginary Happiness is an i. condition HAPPINESS, 3

imitate never failed to i. CHILDREN, 1

immoral the things I really like . . . are either i., illegal, or fattening PLEASURE, 2

immortality I . . . want to achieve i. . . . through not dying DEATH, 2

impossible when you have excluded the i. TRUTH, 4

improbable whatever remains, however i., must be the truth TRUTH, 4

impromptu three weeks to prepare a good i. speech SPEECHES, 21

in you had it i. you CHILDREN, 10

incest except i. and folk-dancing EXPERIENCE, 1

income her Majesty . . . must not . . . look upon me as a source of i. TAXATION, 1
live beyond its i. PROGRESS, 2

indecent It requires one to assume such i. postures SPORT, 13

India I. is a geographical term PLACES, 6

indignation Moral i. is in most cases 2 percent moral MORALITY, 8

indispensables She was one of those i. INDISPENSABILITY, 1

industrial I. relations are like sexual relations WORK, 3

infallible We are none of us i. IMPERFECTION, 3

infanticide as indefensible as i. CENSORSHIP, 3

inferior No one can make you feel i. without your consent INFERIORITY, 1

inform not to i. the reader BUREAUCRACY, 1

injustice threatened with a great i. INJUSTICE, 1
what a man still plans . . . shows the . . . i. in his death DEATH, 4

ink an optimist . . . fills up his crossword puzzle in i. OPTIMISM, 2

innocently i. employed than in getting money MONEY, 5

insect the Egyptians worshipped an i. OCCUPATIONS, 84

inspiration Genius is one per cent i. ACHIEVEMENT, 2

institution more than a game. It's an i. SPORT, 4

insult A man should not i. his wife publicly MARRIAGE, 9

insulted anyone here whom I have not i. SPEECHES, 23

intellects highest i., like the tops of mountains INTELLECT, 3

intellectual i., but I found it too difficult HUMILITY, 3
i. . . . doesn't know how to park a bike INTELLECT, 1

intelligent Each generation imagines itself . . . more i. AGE, 15
stupid are cocksure . . . i. full of doubt DOUBT, 1

intended i. to give you some advice ADVICE, 2

invasion no stand can be made against i. by an idea IDEAS, 2

Ireland English should give I. home rule IRELAND, 6
The problem with I. IRELAND, 4

Irish All races have . . . economists, with the exception of the I. IRELAND, 1
I. . . . devotion to higher arts IRELAND, 1
The I. are a fair people IRELAND, 3

iron the i. has entered his soul
NONCOMMITMENT, 2

irresponsible better to be i. and right
RESPONSIBILITY, 1

irritating differences in taste or opinion are i.
ARGUMENTS, 1

Italy I. a paradise for horses
PLACES, 3

J

jail being in a ship is being in a j.
OCCUPATIONS, 102

jealousies patience with the j. . . . of actors
OCCUPATIONS, 5

Jefferson when Thomas J. dined alone
SPEECHES, 4

Jews The J. and Arabs should . . . settle their differences RELIGION, 1
the J. have made a contribution to the human condition
JEWS, 2

job If two men on the same j. agree
WORK, 11

jockey the . . . cup is given to the j.
INJUSTICE, 2

joke a j. with a double meaning
HUMOUR, 1

jokes Forgive . . . my little j. on Thee
PRAYER, 2
He cannot bear old men's j. AGE, 9

Joneses drag the J. down to my level
FAMILY, 2

journalism Christianity, . . . but why j.
OCCUPATIONS, 57
j. . . . . keeps us in touch with the ignorance of the community
OCCUPATIONS, 64
J. largely consists of saying 'Lord Jones is dead'
OCCUPATIONS, 59
j. what will be grasped at once
OCCUPATIONS, 60

journalists j. put theirs on the front page
OCCUPATIONS, 56

joy A thing of beauty is a j. for ever
BEAUTY, 1
we could never learn to be brave . . . if there were only j.
ENDURANCE, 1

judge duty of a j. is to administer justice
OCCUPATIONS, 65
j. is a law student
OCCUPATIONS, 66
j. is not supposed to know anything about the facts of life
OCCUPATIONS, 67

judgement no one complains of his j.
JUDGMENT, 2
your j. will probably be right
JUDGMENT, 1

judges J. . . . have their lighter moments
OCCUPATIONS, 68

justice duty of a judge is to administer j.
OCCUPATIONS, 65
J. is open to all
JUSTICE, 2
never expected j. from a company
BUSINESS, 10
The j. of my quarrel
JUSTICE, 1

K

kicked he had known many k. down stairs
LEAVING, 7

kind being k. Is all the sad world needs
KINDNESS, 2
I love thee for a heart that's k.
KINDNESS, 1

king He played the K. as though
CRITICISM, 2

kissed Wherever one wants to be k.
WOMEN, 5

knight I never realized that I'd end up being the shortest k. of the year
AWARDS, 3

know all Ye k. on earth
BEAUTY, 2
What you don't k. would make a great book
IGNORANCE, 2

knowledge All k. is of itself of some value
KNOWLEDGE, 3
K. is of two kinds
KNOWLEDGE, 4
province of k. to speak
KNOWLEDGE, 2

L

labour To l. and not ask for any reward
SELFLESSNESS, 1

lack own up to a l. of humour
HUMOUR, 2

lamb to make the lion lie down with the l.
HUMAN NATURE, 2

lamp To keep a l. burning
CHARITY, 3

lamp-post like asking a l. . . . . about dogs
OCCUPATIONS, 35

land they have the l. and we have the Bibles
RELIGION, 4

language The English have no respect for their l.
PLACES, 17

languages she speaks eighteen l. .

And she can't say 'No' in any of them   SEX, 8

last I shall be the l. to go out ·
                                    COURAGE, 1
the l. time that I will take part as
an amateur   FUNERALS, 1

Latin Don't quote L.   SPEECHES, 22
the Devil knows L.   CHILDREN, 8

Latins L. are tenderly enthusiastic
                                    PLACES, 9

laughed Few women care to be l.
at   RIDICULE, 1

laughing Happiness is no l. matter   HAPPINESS, 4
the death of Little Nell without l.
                                INSENSITIVITY, 1
the most fun I ever had without l.
                                    SEX, 2

laughter I was convulsed with l.
                                CRITICISM, 7

law judge is a l. student
                                OCCUPATIONS, 66
The majestic egalitarianism of the
l.   EQUALITY, 1

lawyer Behold a l., an honest man
                                OCCUPATIONS, 72
course to be pursued by a l.
                                OCCUPATIONS, 76
good l. is a bad neighbour
                                OCCUPATIONS, 77
l. in the natural history of mon-
sters   OCCUPATIONS, 74
l. without history or literature
                                OCCUPATIONS, 78

lawyers L. earn a living
                                OCCUPATIONS, 73
l. . . . let out their brains for hire
                                OCCUPATIONS, 70
no bad people . . . no good l.
                                OCCUPATIONS, 71
unfair to believe everything . . .
about l.   OCCUPATIONS, 75

leader I have to follow them, I am
their l.   LEADERSHIP, 2

learn we could never l. to be
brave . . . if there were only joy
                                ENDURANCE, 1

learning L. hath gained most
                                    BOOKS, 3
L. is a treasure   KNOWLEDGE, 5
Their l. is like bread in a besieged
town   PLACES, 13

least death . . . the l. of all evils
                                    DEATH, 3

lechery drink . . . an equivocator
with l.   DRINKING, 14

left You just press the accelerator
to the floor and steer l.   SPORT, 12

legless critic is a l. man
                                OCCUPATIONS, 37

leisure The secret of being miserable is to have l.   SORROW, 2

less l. in this than meets the eye
                                CRITICISM, 1
Specialist – A man who knows
more and more about l. and l.
                                    EXPERTS, 2
the l. they have . . . the more
noise they make   CHARACTER, 1

letter I have made this l. longer
                                VERBOSITY, 1

level-headed When things are
steep, remember to stay l.
                                SELF-CONTROL, 1

levellers Your l. wish to level
down as far as themselves
                                    EQUALITY, 2

liaison l. man and partly P.R.O
                                    BUSINESS, 1

liar Mr. Speaker, I said the honorable member was a l.
                                    APOLOGIES, 2

lie an honest man sent to l. abroad
for . . . his country   DIPLOMACY, 4
L. follows by post   APOLOGIES, 1

life death after l. does greatly
please   DEATH, 8
Football isn't a matter of l. and
death   SPORT, 9
Is l. a boon   MORTALITY, 4
L. is a maze in which we take the
wrong turning   LIFE, 3
L. is a tragedy . . . in close-up
                                    LIFE, 2
L. is like a sewer   LIFE, 4
longest half of your l.   YOUTH, 7
The best part of married l. is the
fights   MARRIAGE, 11
The Book of L. begins
                                WEDDINGS, 23

lightly Angels . . . take themselves
l.   SERIOUSNESS, 1

like I shall not look upon his l.
                                COMPLIMENTS, 4

liked I'm so universally l.
                                POPULARITY, 1

line cancel half a L.   DESTINY, 1

lingerie Brevity is the soul of l.
CLOTHES, 3

lion to make the l. lie down with the lamb HUMAN NATURE, 2

listen privilege of wisdom to l.
KNOWLEDGE, 2

listener A good l. is a good talker with a sore throat SPEECH, 16

literature L. . . . something that will be read twice OCCUPATIONS, 60

Little Nell the death of L. without laughing INSENSITIVITY, 1

live If you l. long enough, the venerability factor creeps in
AGE, 23

l. beyond its income PROGRESS, 2

than to l. up to them PRINCIPLES, 1

living L. frugally, . . . he died early ABSTINENCE, 1

no one has yet found a way to drink for a l. DRINKING, 10

two people l. together for 25 years without having a cross word WEDDINGS, 12

London Dublin, though . . . much worse than L. PLACES, 11

When a man is tired of L.
LONDON, 2

longer I have made this letter l.
VERBOSITY, 1

longest l. half of your life YOUTH, 7

look sit and l. at it for hours
IDLENESS, 2

looks man who l. you . . . in the eye . . . hiding something
INSINCERITY, 1

lord drunk as a l. DRINKING, 12

lordships good enough for their l. on a hot summer afternoon
SPEECHES, 8

lose I shall l. no time in reading it EXCUSES, 2

lost I look upon every day to be l.
FRIENDSHIP, 5

loud A l. noise at one end
CHILDREN, 7

lousy It was kind of l. CRITICISM, 9

love Absence is to l. LEAVING, 4

Alcohol is like l. DRINKING, 5

let brotherly l. continue
HOSPITALITY, 1

L. does not consist in gazing at each other LOVE, 5

L. is blind FRIENDSHIP, 7

L. is moral even without . . . marriage WEDDINGS, 14

L.'s like the measles LOVE, 4

L. . . . the gift of oneself LOVE, 1

l. until after the first attack
LOVE, 3

Many a man has fallen in l. with a girl LOVE, 2

True l.'s the gift which God has given To man alone LOVE, 6

lover easier to be a l. than a husband WEDDINGS, 5

loving But if we stop l. animals
ANIMALS, 4

luck A self-made man . . . believes in l. SELF-MADE MEN, 3

it brings you l. whether you believe . . . or not SUPERSTITION, 1

l., . . . the harder I work the more I have SUPERSTITION, 2

lump a crowd like that . . . brings a l. to my wallet MONEY, 14

lured down which ideas are l. and . . . strangled BUREAUCRACY, 3

M

Macaulay Lord M. SPEECH, 15

machine One m. can do the work of fifty ordinary men
TECHNOLOGY, 2

mad Never go to bed m.
ARGUMENTS, 2

Majesty Her M. is not a subject
ROYALTY, 1

her M. . . . must not . . . look upon me as a source of income
TAXATION, 1

How can I . . . dislike a sex to which Your M. belongs MEN AND WOMEN, 6

majority No candidate . . . elected ex-president by such a large m.
FAILURE, 3

make a Scotsman on the m.
PLACES, 1

maker he adores his m. CONCEIT, 3

malignant the only part of Randolph that was not m. INSULTS, 5

malt M. does more than Milton
DRINKING, 7

man A m. in the house is worth two MEN, 5

A m. is only as old as the woman
AGE, 11

'A was a m., take him for all in all
COMPLIMENTS, 4
follies which a m. regrets the
most   MISTAKES, 4
M. has his will   MEN AND WOMEN, 4
M. is the only animal that can re-
main on friendly terms
HYPOCRISY, 1
rarely . . . one can see in a little
boy the promise of a m.
CHILDREN, 6
The atrocious crime of being a
young m.   YOUTH, 5
The m. who makes no mistakes
MISTAKES, 3
True love's the gift which God
has given To m. alone   LOVE, 6
What's a m.'s first duty
SINCERITY, 3
When a woman behaves like a m.
WOMEN, 7
You cannot make a m. by stand-
ing a sheep   PUBLIC, 1
young m. not yet   WEDDINGS, 4
manners in England people have
good table m.   MANNERS, 1
many what can two do against so
m.   SPEECHES, 25
mark If you would hit the m.
AMBITION, 2
marriage It takes two to make a
m.   WEDDINGS, 19
Love is moral even without . . . m.
WEDDINGS, 14
M. . . . a community . . . making in
all two   MARRIAGE, 1
M. has many pains   MARRIAGE, 2
M. is a wonderful invention
WEDDINGS, 10
M. is popular   WEDDINGS, 20
M. is the only adventure open to
the cowardly   WEDDINGS, 22
m. . . . not a public conveyance
MARRIAGE, 3
m. . . . resembles a pair of shears
MARRIAGE, 7
twenty years of m. make her
something like a public building
MARRIAGE, 10
married A m. couple are well
suited   MARRIAGE, 5
what delight we m. people have
to see   WEDDINGS, 16

marries doesn't much signify
whom one m.   WEDDINGS, 17
marry as easy to m. a rich woman
as a poor woman   WEDDINGS, 21
better to m. than to burn
WEDDINGS, 7
no woman should m. a teetotaller
ABSTINENCE, 6
when a man should m. WEDDINGS, 4
martyrdom M. is the test
FREEDOM, 2
masterpiece Who am I to tamper
with a m.   BOASTS, 7
masters Buy old m.   ART, 3
matinée Robert Houdin who . . .
invented the . . . theater m.
SPEECHES, 26
maturity m. is only a short break
in adolescence   AGE, 8
maunder m. and mumble PUBLIC, 2
May darling buds of M.
COMPLIMENTS, 5
maze Life is a m.   LIFE, 3
measles Love's like the m.
LOVE, 4
medicines Doctors . . . prescribe
m. of which they know little
OCCUPATIONS, 49
meek The m. do not inherit the
earth   HUMILITY, 2
meet Two may talk . . . yet never
really m.   FRIENDSHIP, 2
memorandum A m. is written
BUREAUCRACY, 1
memory Everyone complains of
his m.   JUDGMENT, 2
good storyteller is a person who
has a good m.   SPEECHES, 13
men Great m. are almost always
bad m. . . . .   POWER, 1
It's not the m. in my life that
count   SEX, 10
M. will confess   HUMOUR, 2
schemes o' mice an' m. FAILURE, 1
Why are women . . . so much
more interesting to m.   MEN AND
WOMEN, 9
merger trying to pull off a m. between Heaven and Hell
BUSINESS, 12
mice schemes o' m. an' men
FAILURE, 1
middle people who stay in the m.
of the road   NONCOMMITMENT, 1

mike I'm being amplified by the
m. SPEECHES, 2
militant I am an optimist, unrepentant and m. OPTIMISM, 3
military When the m. man approaches OCCUPATIONS, 105
million man who has a m. dollars
MONEY, 1
Milton after Shakespeare and M.
are forgotten CRITICISM, 8
Malt does more than M. can
DRINKING, 7
mind prodigious quantity of m.
INDECISION, 1
minutes at the rate of sixty m. an
hour TIME, 1
mirror When a man confronts catastrophe . . . a woman looks in
her m. MEN AND WOMEN, 8
miserable The secret of being m.
is to have leisure SORROW, 2
misfortunes strong enough to
bear the m. of others
MISFORTUNE, 2
mistakes The man who makes no
m. MISTAKES, 3
mistresses a better price than old
m. ART, 1
Wives are young men's m.
WEDDINGS, 3
money Brigands demand your m.
or your life WOMEN, 4
except for large sums of m.
RIDICULE, 1
If you can . . . count your m. you
are not . . . rich man MONEY, 4
innocently employed than in getting m. MONEY, 5
M. can't buy friends MONEY, 8
M. is like manure MONEY, 9
M. is like muck MONEY, 2
M., it turned out, was exactly like
sex MONEY, 3
the poor person . . . thinks m.
would help MONEY, 6
When an actor has m.
OCCUPATIONS, 3
You can be young without m.
MONEY, 15
monsters lawyer in the natural
history of m. OCCUPATIONS, 74
moon For years politicians have
promised the m. ACHIEVEMENT, 4

moral Love is m. even without
. . . marriage WEDDINGS, 14
M. indignation is in most cases 2
percent m. MORALITY, 8
m. is what you feel good after
MORALITY, 3
morality M. consists in suspecting
MORALITY, 6
new m. . . . . the old immorality
condoned MORALITY, 7
No m. can be founded on authority MORALITY, 2
more Specialist – A man who
knows m. and m. about less and
less EXPERTS, 2
morn From m. to night, my friend
ENDURANCE, 4
morning 'Tis always m. somewhere BEGINNING, 2
mortal doctor found . . . last disorder m. OCCUPATIONS, 42
mountains highest intellects, like
the tops of m. INTELLECT, 3
mouse leave room for the m.
EXCESS, 1
mouth butter wouldn't melt in her
m. INSULTS, 2
impossible for an Englishman to open
his m. PLACES, 17
moving The M. Finger writes
DESTINY, 1
muck Money is like m. MONEY, 2
mumble maunder and m. PUBLIC, 2
murder men will confess to
treason, m., arson, false teeth
HUMOUR, 2
murdered I m. my grandmother
this morning INATTENTION, 2
music The English may not like
m. MUSIC, 3
The m. teacher came twice each
week MUSIC, 1
Van Gogh's ear for m. INSULTS, 6
mystery a riddle wrapped in a m.
inside an enigma PLACES, 7

N

name-dropper One must not be
a n. SNOBBERY, 2
nation he is the sworn foe of our
n. OCCUPATIONS, 27
No n. was ever ruined by trade
BUSINESS, 3
nearsighted don't raise your

hands because I am also n.
SPEECHES, 1

neck equipping us with a n.
COURAGE, 2

Nell the death of Little N. without
laughing INSENSITIVITY, 1

new There are no n. truths
TRUTH, 6

You suddenly understand something . . . in a n. way EDUCATION, 8

Youth is something very n.
YOUTH, 1

newspaper good n., . . . is a nation talking to itself
OCCUPATIONS, 61

With the n. strike on OBITUARIES, 1

nice amazing how n. people
LEAVING, 2

Be n. to people on your way up
WORK, 7

night From morn to n., my friend
ENDURANCE, 4

Nixon N. . . . would cut down a
redwood tree OCCUPATIONS, 87

no she speaks eighteen languages.
And she can't say 'N.' in any of
them SEX, 8

noise A loud n. at one end
CHILDREN, 7

the less they have . . . the more
n. they make CHARACTER, 1

they . . . love the n. it makes
MUSIC, 3

noisy The people would be just as
n. PUBLIC, 3

nose A custom loathsome to the
eye, hateful to the n. SMOKING, 3

nothing Certainly, there is n. else
here to enjoy PARTIES, 3

doing n. for each other
FRIENDSHIP, 3

from n. to a state of extreme
poverty POVERTY, 2

have n. whatever to do with it
DEATH, 7

N., except my genius BOASTS, 6

When you have n. to say, say n.
SPEECH, 3

novel When I want to read a n.
OCCUPATIONS, 20

nuisance exchange of one n. for
another n. PROGRESS, 3

nurses old men's n. WEDDINGS, 3

O

oaths O. are but words SPEECH, 2

obey born to o. LEADERSHIP, 1

occupation only man . . . apologizing for his o. BUSINESS, 7

odious One is not superior . . . because one sees the world in an
o. light CYNICISM, 1

office not describe holding public
o. LEAVING, 1

o. sanctifies the holder POWER, 1

offspring Heaven has granted me
no o. BOASTS, 5

old Growing o. is like being increasingly penalized AGE, 16

He cannot bear o. men's jokes
AGE, 9

I prefer o. age to the alternative
AGE, 4

man . . . as o. as the woman he
feels AGE, 11

O. men are dangerous AGE, 22

the o. have reminiscences AGE, 18

the o. have rubbed it into the
young that they are wiser AGE, 12

young can do for the o. is to shock
them AGE, 20

older make way for an o. man
LEAVING, 9

to go on getting o. SURVIVAL, 1

one The number o. book . . . was
written by a committee
BUREAUCRACY, 4

one-handed Give me a o. economist ECONOMICS, 3

open I declare this thing o. –
whatever it is SPEECHES, 6

opera o. isn't what it used to be
MUSIC, 5

opinion One often contradicts an
o. ARGUMENTS, 3

opportunities One can present
people with o. OPPORTUNITY, 2

opportunity Equality of o.
OPPORTUNITY, 3

follies . . . he didn't commit when
he had the o. REGRET, 2

optimist an o. . . . fills up his
crossword puzzle in ink
OPTIMISM, 2

I am an o., unrepentant and militant OPTIMISM, 3

The o. proclaims OPTIMISM, 1

oral a terrific story about o. contraception CONTRACEPTION, 1

orators What o. lack in depth SPEECHES, 18

ordering the better o. of the universe UNIVERSE, 1

ordinary One machine can do the work of fifty o. men TECHNOLOGY, 2

organ my second favourite o. SEX, 1

organization a government o. could do it that quickly BUREAUCRACY, 2

overexposure she should catch a cold on o. TRUTH, 3

oyster bold man that first eat an o. COURAGE, 4

P

pain The p. passes, but the beauty remains ENDURANCE, 3

painted Most women are not so young as they are p. WOMEN, 3

painter difficult for a truly creative p. than to paint a rose OCCUPATIONS, 15

never been a boy p. OCCUPATIONS, 13

painters p. who transform the sun into a yellow spot OCCUPATIONS, 17

pants There were times my p. were so thin POVERTY, 5

Your eyes shine like the p. COMPLIMENTS, 2

paper Where were you fellows when the p. was blank OCCUPATIONS, 50

paradise England is a p. for women PLACES, 3

paranoid Even a p. can have enemies ENEMIES, 1

parents by defying their p. and copying one another YOUTH, 2

Don't hold your p. up to contempt FAMILY, 9

From birth to age eighteen, a girl needs good p. AGE, 24

necessary precautions to avoid having p. FAMILY, 1

P. . . . a disappointment to their children FAMILY, 6

P. learn a lot from their children CHILDREN, 13

the way p. obey their children FAMILY, 10

Parliament P. is the longest running farce GOVERNMENT, 2

parting P. is such sweet sorrow LEAVING, 12

party best number for a dinner p. is two PARTIES, 2

pass I shall not p. this way again MORTALITY, 6

young have aspirations that never come to p. AGE, 18

past Even God cannot change the p. PAST, 2

Keep off your thoughts from things that are p. PAST, 6

people who live in the p. PROGRESS, 1

The only thing I regret about my p. life AGE, 2

The p., at least, is secure PAST, 7

The p. is a foreign country PAST, 3

The p. is the only dead thing . PAST, 5

what's p. help Should be p. grief REGRET, 3

patient good p. is one who OCCUPATIONS, 44

patients Doctors think a lot of p. are cured OCCUPATIONS, 43

patriot He was a great p. . . . provided . . . that he really is dead COMPLIMENTS, 9

patriotism P. is the last refuge PATRIOTISM, 2

pay better . . . not vow, than . . . vow and not p. PROMISES, 1

peace *P*. . . . a period of cheating PEACE, 1

peerage When I want a p., I shall buy one AWARDS, 2

pen less brilliant p. than mine BOASTS, 1

people Be nice to p. on your way up WORK, 7

It is with . . . p. as with . . . bottles CHARACTER, 1

p. attached to cats ANIMALS, 4

p. who stay in the middle of the road NONCOMMITMENT, 1

The Lord prefers common-looking p. APPEARANCE, 5

The p. would be just as noisy PUBLIC, 3

You can fool too many of the p.
DECEPTION, 3

perfection P. has one grave defect
PERFECTION, 1

performance it takes away the p.
DRINKING, 14

perils smile at p. past PAST, 4

perish better to p. than to continue schoolmastering
OCCUPATIONS, 113

perversion that melancholy sexual p. known as continence
ABSTINENCE, 5

pervert Once: a philosopher; twice: a p. DEBAUCHERY, 2

pessimist the p. fears this is true
OPTIMISM, 1

philosopher never yet p. That could endure the toothache
ENDURANCE, 5

Once: a p.; twice: a pervert
DEBAUCHERY, 2

physicians the help of too many p. MEDICINE, 1

Piccadilly Crossing P. Circus
LONDON, 3

pickle weaned on a p.
APPEARANCE, 6

pimp editor should have a p. for a brother OCCUPATIONS, 51

piss I can p. the old boy BOASTS, 4

place Home is the p. where
HOME, 2

planet it fell on the wrong p.
WEAPONS, 1

plans what a man still p. . . . shows the . . . injustice in his death DEATH, 4

plays p. about rape, sodomy and drug addiction THEATRE, 1

playwright drama critic is a person who surprises the p.
OCCUPATIONS, 36

please I . . . do what I p.
FREEDOM, 1

They . . . say what they p.
FREEDOM, 1

pleasure gave p. to the spectators
MORALITY, 4

p. of fishing them out again
FRIENDSHIP, 9

pleasures One half . . . cannot understand the p. PLEASURE, 1

pocket To be played with both hands in the p. MUSIC, 7

poem I do not think this p. will reach its destination CRITICISM, 10

poetry read a little p. sometimes
IGNORANCE, 1

police I'm not against the p.
OCCUPATIONS, 81

policemen P. are numbered
OCCUPATIONS, 82

politeness Punctuality is the p. of kings PROMPTNESS, 1

politician at home you're just a p.
OCCUPATIONS, 85

politics P. come from man.
OCCUPATIONS, 91

P. is the art of preventing people from taking part OCCUPATIONS, 89

p. was the second lowest profession OCCUPATIONS, 86

poor only the p. . . . are forbidden to beg POVERTY, 1

p. have no right to the property of the rich POVERTY, 3

the p. person . . . thinks money would help MONEY, 6

posterity doing something for p.
PAST, 1

postures It requires one to assume such indecent p. SPORT, 13

poultry A p. matter MONEY, 7

poverty from nothing to a state of extreme p. POVERTY, 2

power Men of p. have not time to read POWER, 4

P. tends to corrupt POWER, 1

wrong sort of people are always in p. POWER, 8

You only have p. over people
POWER, 5

powers Headmasters have p.
OCCUPATIONS, 114

practiced A genius! For thirty-seven years I've p. . . . and now they call me a genius
ACHIEVEMENT, 5

praise To refuse p. PRAISE, 2

praising advantage of . . . p. . . . oneself PRAISE, 1

pray p. for you at St Paul's
PRAYER, 3

prejudice I am free of all p.
HATE, 1

prejudices Common sense is the collection of p. PREJUDICE, 1

President American . . . prepared to run for P. OCCUPATIONS, 90

one thing about being P. POWER, 3

pretty There's only one p. child CHILDREN, 12

preventing Politics is the art of p. people from taking part OCCUPATIONS, 89

price a better p. than old mistresses ART, 3

the p. of everything and the value of nothing CYNICISM, 2

princes mine were p. of the earth JEWS, 1

principle agree to a thing in p. AGREEMENT, 1

except from some strong p. PRINCIPLES, 3

the p. seems the same PLACES, 4

principles easier to fight for one's p. PRINCIPLES, 1

Whenever two good people argue over p. PRINCIPLES, 2

print big p. giveth BUSINESS, 8

printers those books by which the p. have lost BOOKS, 3

prison Anyone who has been to . . . public school will . . . feel . . . at home in p. EDUCATION, 12

prisoners If this is the way Queen Victoria treats her p. COMPLAINTS, 2

privacy That should assure us of . . . forty-five minutes of undisturbed p. INATTENTION, 1

P.R.O liaison man and partly P. BUSINESS, 1

professor p. of poetry is rather like being a Kentucky colonel OCCUPATIONS, 111

profit Drop . . . what tomorrow may bring . . . count as p. every day that Fate allows you PRESENT, 2

progress All p. is based PROGRESS, 2

What we call p. is PROGRESS, 3

prohibition Communism is like p. COMMUNISM, 1

promise A p. made is a debt unpaid PROMISES, 2

rarely . . . one can see in a little boy the p. of a man CHILDREN, 6

pronounce p. foreign names as he chooses PRONUNCIATION, 1

property poor have no right to the p. of the rich POVERTY, 3

prophecies bring about the verification of his own p. PROPHECY, 1

prosper Treason doth never p. BETRAYAL, 2

protect p. the writer BUREAUCRACY, 1

proud no guarantee . . . you will not be p. of the feat HUMILITY, 1

prudence freedom of speech, freedom of conscience, and the p. never to practise . . . them FREEDOM, 7

psychiatrist A p. is a man who goes to the Folies-Bergère OCCUPATIONS, 95

P.: A man who asks you a lot of expensive questions OCCUPATIONS, 92

see a p. out of boredom OCCUPATIONS, 94

public a more mean, stupid . . . ungrateful animal than the p. PUBLIC, 4

give the p. what they want to see and they'll come out for it FUNERALS, 5

not describe holding p. office LEAVING, 1

The P. is an old woman PUBLIC, 2

twenty years of marriage make her . . . like a p. building MARRIAGE, 10

public school Anyone who has been to . . . p. will . . . feel . . . at home in prison EDUCATION, 12

pulse worse occupations . . . than feeling a woman's p. OCCUPATIONS, 47

punctuality P. is the politeness of kings PROMPTNESS, 1

P. is the virtue of the bored PROMPTNESS, 2

punished Am I not p. enough in not being born an Englishman PLACES, 20

punishing p. anyone who comes between them MARRIAGE, 8

reward The r. of a thing well
done   SUCCESS, 3
To labour and not ask for any r.
                    SELFLESSNESS, 1
rich as easy to marry a r. woman
as a poor woman   WEDDINGS, 21
as well off as if he were r.
                    MONEY, 1
If you can . . . count your money
you are not . . . r. man MONEY, 4
poor have no right to the property of the r.   POVERTY, 3
the wretchedness of being r.
                    MONEY, 12
you have to live with r. people
                    MONEY, 12
riddle a r. wrapped in a mystery
inside an enigma   PLACES, 7
right better to be irresponsible
and r.   RESPONSIBILITY, 1
Every man has a r. to utter what
he thinks truth   FREEDOM, 2
I disapprove of what you say, but
I will defend . . . your r. to say it
                    FREEDOM, 8
our country, r. or wrong
                    PATRIOTISM, 1
ring Don't carry away that arm till
I have . . . my r.   PRACTICALITY, 1
Ritz like the R. hotel   JUSTICE, 2
road Does the r. wind up-hill
                    ENDURANCE, 4
robbed when you've r. a man of
everything   POWER, 5
romance Twenty years of r.
makes a woman look like a ruin
                    MARRIAGE, 10
room There is always r. at the
top   AMBITION, 5
who sneaked into my r. at three
o'clock this morning COMPLAINTS, 1
rose difficult for a truly creative
painter than to paint a r.
                    OCCUPATIONS, 15
rosebuds Gather ye r. while ye
may   PRESENT, 1
roses days of wine and r.
                    MORTALITY, 1
I would like my r. to see you
                    COMPLIMENTS, 6
ruin Twenty years of romance
makes a woman look like a r.
                    MARRIAGE, 10

rule A little r., a little sway
                    MORTALITY, 3
English should give Ireland home
r.   IRELAND, 6

S

sad being kind Is all the s. world
needs   KINDNESS, 2
safety s. is in our speed HASTE, 1
said they do not know what they
have s.   SPEECHES, 12
sailor wonder . . . sane man can be
a s.   OCCUPATIONS, 101
sailors s. get money like horses
                OCCUPATIONS, 106
salad My s. days   YOUTH, 6
salary s. of the chief executive
. . . not a market award for
achievement   BUSINESS, 4
same principle seems the s.
                    PLACES, 4
Samuel When they circumcised
Herbert S.   INSULTS, 2
sardines Life is . . . like a tin of s.
                    LIFE, 1
sat The . . . gentleman has s. so
long on the fence
                NONCOMMITMENT, 2
Saviour But it's 'S. of 'is country'
when the guns OCCUPATIONS, 103
say cannot s. what you have to s.
in twenty minutes SPEECHES, 10
s. what you have to s., and then
sit down   SPEECHES, 22
They are to s. what they please
                    FREEDOM, 1
they do not know what they are
going to s.   SPEECHES, 12
When you have nothing to s.
                    SPEECH, 3
saying when . . . speaking, they do
not know what they are s.
                    SPEECHES, 12
scarce S., sir. Mighty s.
                    WOMEN, 11
scene artist who always paints the
same s. pleases the public
                OCCUPATIONS, 19
schemes best laid s. o' mice an'
men   FAILURE, 1
school never gone to s. may steal
from a freight car EDUCATION, 9
nothing on earth . . . so horrible as
a s.   EDUCATION, 10

silence dangerous to an author as s. OCCUPATIONS, 24
occasional flashes of s. SPEECH, 15
S. is as full of potential wisdom SPEECH, 9
That man's s. is wonderful to listen to SPEECH, 8
sin beauty is only s. deep BEAUTY, 5
single a s. man in possession of a good fortune must be in want of a wife WEDDINGS, 2
sit nobody can tell you when to s. down POWER, 3
say what you have to say, and then s. down SPEECHES, 22
sitting I do most of my work s. down HUMOUR, 4
sixty at the rate of s. minutes an hour TIME, 1
size I am not this s., really SPEECHES, 2
skating s. over thin ice HASTE, 1
slush pure as the driven s. PURITY, 1
smaller accepts a s. as a favour INJUSTICE, 1
smells the only dead thing that s. sweet PAST, 5
smile s. at perils past PAST, 4
smoke no woman should marry ...a man who does not s. ABSTINENCE, 6
resembling the horrible Stygian s. of the pit SMOKING, 3
smoking resolve to give up s., drinking and loving ABSTINENCE, 4
s. cigars... before, after, and if need be during all meals SMOKING, 2
snore s. and you sleep alone SLEEP, 1
Snow White I used to be S. PURITY, 4
sober How do you look when I'm s. CLOTHES, 2
one sees in Garbo s. COMPLIMENTS, 8
soldier Drinking is the s.'s pleasure OCCUPATIONS, 100
worse the man the better the s. OCCUPATIONS, 104
soldiers S. in peace are like OCCUPATIONS, 99

solicitor s. is a man who OCCUPATIONS, 69
some You can fool s. of the people all the time DECEPTION, 2
someone I wouldn't be... talking to s. like you SNOBBERY, 1
somewhere 'Tis always morning s. BEGINNING, 2
sorrow Parting is such sweet s. LEAVING, 12
soul Education is... the s. of a society EDUCATION, 3
the... essence of a human s. BOOKS, 2
the iron has entered his s. NONCOMMITMENT, 2
soup concludes that it will... make better s. IDEALISM, 2
source her Majesty... must not ...look upon me as a s. of income TAXATION, 1
sparrow It is a city where you can see a s. fall IRELAND, 5
speak Begin low, s. slow SPEECHES, 7
I only s. right on SPEECHES, 20
province of knowledge to s. KNOWLEDGE, 2
time to think before I s. SPEECH, 4
speaking Adepts in the s. trade SPEECHES, 11
when... s., they do not know what they are saying SPEECHES, 12
specialist S. – A man who knows more and more about less and less EXPERTS, 2
speech A s. is like a love affair SPEECHES, 17
freedom of s., freedom of conscience, and the prudence never to practise... them FREEDOM, 7
I dreamt that I was making a s. SPEECHES, 14
indignation makes an excellent s. SPEECHES, 15
let thy s. be short SPEECHES, 9
The most precious things in s. SPEECH, 13
The true use of s. SPEECH, 6
three weeks to prepare a good impromptu s. SPEECHES, 21
speechmaker fellow who says, 'I'm no s.' SPEECHES, 16
speed safety is in our s. HASTE, 1

spoon S. feeding . . . teaches us
nothing but the shape of the s.
EDUCATION, 7

sport man wants to murder a tiger he calls it s. HUNTING, 4
the s. of kings HUNTING, 6

sportsman destroys one of the
works of God we call him a s.
HUNTING, 3

spurts They move forward in s.
CHILDREN, 3

stairs he had known many kicked
down s. LEAVING, 7

star Being a s. has made it possible FAME, 2

stars Clad in the beauty of a thousand s. BEAUTY, 3

statesman abroad you're a s.
OCCUPATIONS, 85

statue there's a s. inside every
block of stone OBESITY, 2

stealth Do good by s. GOOD, 3

steel arm'd with more than complete s. JUSTICE, 1

steep When things are s., remember to stay level-headed SELF-
CONTROL, 1

steer You just press the accelerator to the floor and s. left
SPORT, 12

step only the first s. . . . is difficult
BEGINNING, 1

stick meant us to s. it out
COURAGE, 2

sticks Casting a ball at three
straight s. SPORT, 5

stomach use a little wine for thy
s.'s sake DRINKING, 4
You can't think rationally on an
empty s. THINKING, 2

stops The buck s. here
RESPONSIBILITY, 2

story interesting thing about any
s. OCCUPATIONS, 63

storyteller good s. is a person
who has a good memory
SPEECHES, 13

strange pass my declining years
saluting s. women AGE, 13

strangled down which ideas are
lured and . . . s. BUREAUCRACY, 3

streets S. full of water PLACES, 2

strong s. enough to bear the misfortunes of others MISFORTUNE, 2

study much s. is a weariness of
the flesh BOOKS, 1

stuff The future is made of the
same s. FUTURE, 5

stupid At sixteen I was s., confused
AGE, 8
s. are cocksure . . . intelligent full of
doubt DOUBT, 1

Stygian resembling the horrible S.
smoke of the pit SMOKING, 3

subject Her Majesty is not a s.
ROYALTY, 1
poetry . . . not really a s. one can
profess OCCUPATIONS, 111

succeed It is not enough to s.
RUTHLESSNESS, 3

success a self-made man who
owed his lack of s. to nobody
SELF-MADE MEN, 2
I thought that s. spelled happiness
HAPPINESS, 2
no very lively hope of s. PRAYER, 3
only place where s. comes before
work SUCCESS, 4
The penalty of s. SUCCESS, 1
two to make a marriage a s.
WEDDINGS, 19

successful It was very s.
WEAPONS, 1

suit in a light so dim he would not
have chosen a s. by it LOVE, 2

suitable no s. material to work on
LEADERSHIP, 1

summons when Fate s.
MORTALITY, 2

sun Fear no more the heat o' the s.
LEAVING, 11

superior One is not s. . . . because one sees the world in an
odious light CYNICISM, 1

superstitions s. of the human
mind PURITY, 3

support s. me when I am . . .
wrong SUPPORT, 1

swan What time is the next s.
MISTAKES, 5

sway A little rule, a little s.
MORTALITY, 3

T

tailor I go to a better t. than any
of you CLOTHES, 1

take They have to t. you in
HOME, 2

against fame . . . has the author's name on the t.   HYPOCRISY, 2

tobacco who lives without t.
.   SMOKING, 4

today Its history dates from t.
ROYALTY, 2

together two people living t. for 25 years without having a cross word   WEDDINGS, 12

toil To t. and not to seek for rest
SELFLESSNESS, 1

tomorrow Drop . . . what t. may bring . . . count as profit every day that Fate allows you
PRESENT, 2

tongue One t. is sufficient for a woman   WOMEN, 10

Tony T. . . . he immatures with age   INSULTS, 7

toothache man with t. . . . teeth are sound   ENVY, 1
philosopher that could endure the t.   ENDURANCE, 5

top I started at the t. and worked my way down   ACHIEVEMENT, 7
There is always room at the t.
AMBITION, 5

torch Truth, like a t.   TRUTH, 5

trade No nation was ever ruined by t.   BUSINESS, 3
same t. . . . conversation ends in a conspiracy   BUSINESS, 9

travels A man t. the world over
HOME, 3

treason T. doth never prosper
BETRAYAL, 2

true Mr. Speaker, I said the honorable member was a liar it is t. and I am sorry for it APOLOGIES, 2

trust Never t. a husband too far
WEDDINGS, 18

truth a t. universally acknowledged   WEDDINGS, 2
Beauty is t., t. beauty   BEAUTY, 2
Every man has a right to utter what he thinks t.   FREEDOM, 2
facts must never get in the way of t.   OCCUPATIONS, 58
It takes two to speak the t.
TRUTH, 7
Some men love t. so much
TRUTH, 3
the t. shall make you free
TRUTH, 2

T., like a torch   TRUTH, 5
t. that makes men free   TRUTH, 1
whatever remains, however improbable, must be the t. TRUTH, 4
writers regard t. as their most valuable possession
OCCUPATIONS, 26

truths There are no new t.
TRUTH, 6

try t. everything once
EXPERIENCE, 1

tunnel light at the end of the t.
. . . of an oncoming train
PESSIMISM, 2

turn I wouldn't have left a t. unstoned   CRITICISM, 11
world would begin to t. the other way   PROGRESS, 1

turning Life is a maze in which we take the wrong t.   LIFE, 3

twenty the first t. years YOUTH, 7

twenty-one confidence of t.
YOUTH, 4

twice desire to be praised t. over
PRAISE, 2
Literature . . . something that will be read t.   OCCUPATIONS, 60

two It takes t. to speak the truth
TRUTH, 7
what can t. do against so many
SPEECHES, 25

U

unanimity Our agenda is now exhausted. . . . we find ourselves in such complete u.   AGREEMENT, 2

underdogs never find an Englishman among the u.   PLACES, 21

understand child of five would u. this   SIMPLICITY, 1
if he could make *me* u. . . . it would be clear to all
UNDERSTANDING, 1
You suddenly u. something . . . in a new way   EDUCATION, 8

understanding Most men . . . give evidence against their own u.   SPEECH, 7

uneatable the unspeakable in full pursuit of the u.   HUNTING, 7

uneducated Democracy . . . government by the u.   DEMOCRACY, 2

unfaithful better to be u.
ADULTERY, 1

universe take his attention away
from the u.　PRAYER, 1
the better ordering of the u.
UNIVERSE, 1

unpaid A promise made is a debt
u.　PROMISES, 2

unspeakable the u. in full pursuit
of the uneatable　HUNTING, 7

unstoned I wouldn't have left a
turn u.　CRITICISM, 11

unused left over from last year u.
ADVICE, 2

up I saw it at a disadvantage –
the curtain was u.　CRITICISM, 12

use What is the u. of a new-born
child　TECHNOLOGY, 1

useless most beautiful things . . .
are the most u.　BEAUTY, 4

V

valet difference between a man
and his v.　OCCUPATIONS, 97

value All knowledge is of itself of
some v.　KNOWLEDGE, 3
the price of everything and the v.
of nothing　CYNICISM, 2

values ideas are of more importance than v.　INTELLECT, 2

Van Gogh V.'s ear for music
INSULTS, 6

variety custom stale her infinite v.
COMPLIMENTS, 3

venerability If you live long
enough, the v. factor creeps in
AGE, 23

verification bring about the v. of
his own prophecies　PROPHECY, 1

verse no v. can give pleasure . . .
that is written by drinkers of
water　DRINKING, 6

vestry I will see you in the v. after service　OCCUPATIONS, 29

vice This v. brings in one hundred
million francs . . . every year
SMOKING, 5

victims Man is the only animal
. . . on friendly terms with the v.
. . . he eats　HYPOCRISY, 1

Victoria If this is the way Queen
V. treats her prisoners
COMPLAINTS, 2

virginity that v. could be a virtue
PURITY, 3

virtue name a v. that brings in as
much revenue　SMOKING, 5
to practise five things . . . constitutes perfect v.　VIRTUE, 1

virtues No one gossips about . . .
secret v.　GOSSIP, 1

voice The higher the v.
INTELLECT, 4

vow better . . . not v., than . . . v.
and not pay　PROMISES, 1

vulgar Arguments . . . v. and often
unconvincing　ARGUMENTS, 6

W

wages Home art gone and ta'en
thy w.　LEAVING, 11

Wagstaff a disgrace to our family
name of W.　FAMILY, 4

waiting w. for the cock to crow
BETRAYAL, 3

walk Golf is a good w. spoiled
SPORT, 11

walks She w. in beauty
COMPLIMENTS, 1

wallet a crowd like that . . . brings
a lump to my w.　MONEY, 14

want give the public what they w.
to see and they'll come out for it
FUNERALS, 5

war When the rich wage w.
POVERTY, 4

water no verse can give pleasure
. . . that is written by drinkers of
w.　DRINKING, 6
Streets full of w.　PLACES, 2
w. flowed like champagne
ABSTINENCE, 3
w. still keeps falling over PLACES, 1

way woman has her w.　MEN AND
WOMEN, 5

wayside If you see anybody fallen
by the w.　CHARITY, 2

weak Idleness . . . the refuge of
w. minds　IDLENESS, 1

wealth God shows his contempt
for w.　MONEY, 10
W. is like sea-water　FAME, 4

weaned w. on a pickle
APPEARANCE, 6

weariness much study is a w. of
the flesh　BOOKS, 1

wedding A man looks pretty
small at a w.　WEDDINGS, 24

weed What is a w.　GOOD, 2

weep w. for her sins at the other
ADULTERY, 2

welcome Advice is seldom w.
ADVICE, 1

well as w. off as if he were rich
MONEY, 1

reward of a thing w. done
SUCCESS, 3

wheat An editor . . . separates
the w. from the chaff
OCCUPATIONS, 53

when w. a man should marry
WEDDINGS, 4

where W. were you fellows when
the paper was blank
OCCUPATIONS, 50

white I used to be Snow W.
PURITY, 4

When the w. man came we had
the land
RELIGION, 3

White House gathered together
at the W.
SPEECHES, 4

who w. you are, you aren't anybody
FAME, 3

widow you, my dear, will be my
w.
JEALOUSY, 1

wife A loving w. will do anything
MARRIAGE, 4

A man should not insult his w.
publicly
MARRIAGE, 9

remorse for what you have
thought about your w.
MARRIAGE, 6

single man . . . must be in want of
a w.
WEDDINGS, 2

The husband frae the w. despises
WEDDINGS, 8

with a w. to tell him what to do
WORK, 6

will His right was clear, his w.
was strong
RIGHT, 1

Man has his w. MEN AND WOMEN, 5

We have to believe in free w.
FREEDOM, 6

will-power There is no such thing
as a great talent without great
w.
ACHIEVEMENT, 1

wind what w. is to fire LEAVING, 4

words but w.
SPEECH, 2

wine days of w. and roses
MORTALITY, 1

use a little w. for thy stomach's
sake
DRINKING, 4

wisdom in much w. is much grief
WISDOM, 1

privilege of w. to listen
KNOWLEDGE, 2

Silence is . . . full of potential w.
SPEECH, 9

wise a w. father FAMILY, 7

wiser Be w. than other people
WISDOM, 2

the old have rubbed it into the
young that they are w. AGE, 12

wish most . . . w. they were the
only one alive CONCEIT, 1

wit Brevity is the soul of ˜w.
SPEECHES, 19

I have neither w., nor words, nor
worth
SPEECHES, 20

wither Age cannot w. her
COMPLIMENTS, 3

wives husbands and w. . . . belong
to different sexes MEN AND
WOMEN, 1

The others were only my w.
JEALOUSY, 1

W. are young men's mistresses
WEDDINGS, 3

woman A diplomat . . . always remembers a w.'s birthday AGE, 10

A man is only as old as the w.
AGE, 11

Any w. who understands the
problems of running a home
OCCUPATIONS, 88

It's a sort of bloom on a w.
CHARM, 1

Once a w. has given you her
heart
WOMEN, 12

one can . . . see in a little girl the
threat of a w. CHILDREN, 6

One tongue is sufficient for a w.
WOMEN, 10

Twenty years of romance makes
a w. look like a ruin MARRIAGE, 10

When a w. behaves like a man
WOMEN, 7

w. has her way MEN AND WOMEN, 5

w. seldom asks advice WOMEN, 1

W. will be the last thing civilized
by Man
WOMEN, 9

women Few w. care to be
laughed at
RIDICULE, 1

proper function of w. WOMEN, 6

Why are w. . . . so much more interesting to men   MEN AND WOMEN, 9
w. . . . not so young as . . . painted   WOMEN, 3
w. require both   WOMEN, 4
word Good isn't the w.   CRITICISM, 3
Nor all thy Tears wash out a W.   DESTINY, 1
words neither wit, nor w., nor worth   SPEECHES, 20
W. are . . . the most powerful drug   SPEECH, 11
w. but wind   SPEECH, 2
w. once spoke . . . never be re-call'd   SPEECH, 14
You can stroke people with w.   SPEECH, 5
work I like w.; it fascinates me   IDLENESS, 2
no w., nor device, nor knowledge . . . in the grave   WORK, 2
only place where success comes before w.   SUCCESS, 4
W. is the curse of the drinking classes   WORK, 10
world A man travels the w. over   HOME, 3
good deed in a naughty w.   GOOD, 4
I . . . pass through this w. but once   MORTALITY, 6
joy that a man is born into the w.   CHILDREN, 2
the w., the flesh, and the devil   OCCUPATIONS, 62
worlds we live in the best of all possible w.   OPTIMISM, 1
worse Dublin, though . . . much w. than London   PLACES, 11
worth W. seeing? yes   IRELAND, 2
worthy give the teachers stipends w. of the pains   OCCUPATIONS, 117
is not w. to live   SMOKING, 4
wounds To fight and not to heed the w.   SELFLESSNESS, 1
writer Asking a working w. . . . about critics   OCCUPATIONS, 35
best way to become a successful w.   OCCUPATIONS, 22
protect the w.   BUREAUCRACY, 1

writers w. regard truth as their most valuable possession   OCCUPATIONS, 26
writes Moving Finger w.   DESTINY, 1
wrong A door is what a dog is . . . on the w. side of   DOGS, 2
Of course not . . . I may be w.   UNCERTAINTY, 1
our country, right or w.   PATRIOTISM, 1
responsible and w.   RESPONSIBILITY, 1
support me when I am . . . w.   SUPPORT, 1
Yes, once . . . I thought I had made a w. decision   MISTAKES, 2
wrote blockhead ever w. except for money   OCCUPATIONS, 25

Y

yacht I had to sink my y. to make my guests go home   PARTIES, 1
yet A young man not y.   WEDDINGS, 4
but not y.   MORALITY, 1
young aged diplomats . . . bored than for y. men to die   DIPLOMACY, 1
All that the y. can do for the old   AGE, 20
Most women are not so y. as they are painted   WOMEN, 3
The atrocious crime of being a y. man   YOUTH, 5
the old have rubbed it into the y. that they are wiser   AGE, 12
The y. always have the same problem   YOUTH, 2
The y. have aspirations   AGE, 18
to make me y. again   SURVIVAL, 1
You can be y. without money   MONEY, 15
youngest not even the y. of us   IMPERFECTION, 3
youth Y. is something very new   YOUTH, 1
Y. will come . . . beat on my door   YOUTH, 3

NAME INDEX

Brahms, Johannes SPEECHES, 23
Brancusi, Constantin EXCUSES, 1
Braun, Wernher von WEAPONS, 1
Brenan, Gerald INTELLECT, 2
Brien, Alan BOASTS, 2
Browning, Robert AGE, 3;
AMBITION, 1
Buck, Pearl FAITH, 1
Burgess, Anthony SLEEP, 1
Burghley, William Cecil, Lord
OCCUPATIONS, 99
Burns, Robert FAILURE, 1;
OCCUPATIONS, 33; WEDDINGS, 8
Burton, Richard OCCUPATIONS, 2
Burton, Robert PLACES, 3
Bussy-Rabutin LEAVING, 4
Butler, Samuel DOGS, 1; HYPOCRISY,
1; PRAISE, 1; PROGRESS, 2; SPEECH, 2;
TRUTH, 3; WOMEN, 4
Byron, Henry James GAMES, 2
Byron, Lord COMPLIMENTS, 1;
LEAVING, 5

C

Cabell, James OPTIMISM, 1;
PESSIMISM, 1
Cameron, James OCCUPATIONS, 58
Campbell, Thomas OCCUPATIONS,
27
Canetti, Elias DEATH, 4
Carey, George RELIGION, 2
Carlyle, Jane Welsh INJUSTICE, 1
Carlyle, Thomas BOOKS, 2;
OCCUPATIONS, 113; PUBLIC, 2
Carrington, Lord SCIENCE, 1
Carter, Jimmy BUREAUCRACY, 2
Cartland, Barbara SNOBBERY, 1
Cary, Joyce ADULTERY, 2; ART, 2
Catherwood, Mary FRIENDSHIP, 2
Chamfort, Nicolas INGRATITUDE, 1
Chamfort, Sébastien
OCCUPATIONS, 40
Chandler, Raymond APPEARANCE,
1; DRINKING, 5
Chanel, Coco WOMEN, 5; YOUTH, 1
Chaplin, Charlie LIFE, 2
Chateaubriand, Vicomte de
CYNICISM, 1
Chekhov, Anton OCCUPATIONS, 3
Chesterfield, Earl of ADVICE, 1;
IDLENESS, 1; WISDOM, 2
Chesterton, G. K. DEMOCRACY, 2;
EDUCATION, 3; GOOD, 1; OCCUPATIONS,
59; SERIOUSNESS, 1; SPEECHES, 2

Chevalier, Maurice AGE, 4; LOVE, 2
Christie, Agatha WEDDINGS, 9
Churchill, Charles SPEECHES, 11
Churchill, Winston DIPLOMACY, 2;
OCCUPATIONS, 114; PLACES, 4, 5, 6, 7;
PRONUNCIATION, 1; RESPONSIBILITY, 1;
SMOKING, 2; SPEECHES, 12; SPORT, 1
Ciardi, John OCCUPATIONS, 12
Clemenceau, Georges AGE, 5
Cobb, Irvin S. SPEECHES, 13
Cocks, Barnett BUREAUCRACY, 3
Colby, Frank More HUMOUR, 2
Coleridge, Samuel Taylor
SINCERITY, 1
Colette SEX, 4
Collins, Joan MEN, 1
Colton, Charles Caleb EDUCATION,
4; SPEECH, 3
Compton-Burnett, Ivy
LEADERSHIP, 1
Conan Doyle, Arthur TRUTH, 4
Confucius IMPERFECTION, 1; VIRTUE,
1
Connolly, Billy WEDDINGS, 10
Connolly, Cyril CHILDREN, 3; LIFE, 3;
OCCUPATIONS, 60
Constable, John OCCUPATIONS, 13
Cook, Peter THEATRE, 1
Corneille, Pierre GIFTS, 1; SORROW,
1
Coward, Noël HUMOUR, 5; MUSIC, 5
Crabbe, George OCCUPATIONS, 54
Crisp, Quentin FAMILY, 1, 2; PRAYER,
1; YOUTH, 2
Cromwell, Oliver PUBLIC, 3
Crosby, Bing FRIENDSHIP, 3
Curzon, Lord MISTAKES, 1

D

Daley, Janet RUTHLESSNESS, 1
Daniels, R. G. APPEARANCE, 2
Darrow, Clarence Seward
CLOTHES, 1
Darwin, Erasmus SPEECH, 4
Davies, W. H. ABSTINENCE, 2;
KINDNESS, 1
Davis, Bette MEN, 2; OBITUARIES, 1;
SEX, 5
Davis Jnr, Sammy FAME, 2
Davy, Humphry ART, 5
Day, Clarence Shepard FUNERALS,
2
Decatur, Stephen PATRIOTISM, 1

Goldsmith, Oliver
BOOKS, 4; BUSINESS, 5; OCCUPATIONS, 42;
SPEECH, 6
Gosse, Edmund CRITICISM, 4
Grace, W. G. SPORT, 3
Grade, Lew BOASTS, 3
Gray, Thomas MORTALITY, 5
Grellet, Stephen MORTALITY, 6
Guitry, Sacha JEALOUSY, 1
Gulbenkian, Nubar PARTIES, 2

H

Halifax, Lord LEAVING, 7; SPEECH, 7
Hall, Jerry WOMEN, 8
Hamilton, William TRUTH, 5
Hampton, Christopher
OCCUPATIONS, 35
Hardy, Thomas SPEECH, 8
Harington, John BETRAYAL, 2
Harris, George ADVICE, 2
Hartley, L. P. PAST, 3
Hazlitt, William PUBLIC, 4; THINKING,
1
Heine, Heinrich CENSORSHIP, 1;
OCCUPATIONS, 23
Heller, Joseph SELF-MADE MEN, 2
Hemingway, Ernest MORALITY, 3;
PLACES, 10
Herbert, A. P. WEDDINGS, 12
Herford, Oliver OCCUPATIONS, 6
Herold, Don OCCUPATIONS, 43
Herrick, Robert PRESENT, 1
Hitchcock, Alfred OCCUPATIONS, 81
Hitler, Adolf PUBLIC, 5
Hockney, David OCCUPATIONS, 14
Holmes, Oliver Wendell
KNOWLEDGE, 2; MEN AND WOMEN, 5;
OCCUPATIONS, 44; WISDOM, 3
Hope, Anthony IGNORANCE, 1
Hope, Bob SPEECHES, 24
Horace DRINKING, 6; PRESENT, 2;
SELF-CONTROL, 1
Horne, Richard Henry BEGINNING,
2
Housman, A. E. DRINKING, 7
Howe, E. W. FRIENDSHIP, 4
Hubbard, Elbert TECHNOLOGY, 2
Hubbard, F. McKinney SPEECHES,
16
Hughes, Thomas SPORT, 4
Hughes, William Morris BETRAYAL,
3
Hugo, Victor IDEAS, 2

Huneker, James G. OCCUPATIONS,
73
Huxley, Aldous ABSTINENCE, 5;
APPEARANCE, 4; INDISPENSABILITY, 1;
SINCERITY, 2; SPEECH, 9

I

Ibsen, Henrik SINCERITY, 3; YOUTH, 3

J

James I SMOKING, 3
Jarry, Alfred CHIVALRY, 2
Jerome, Jerome K. IDLENESS, 2
Jerrold, Douglas William LOVE, 4
Johnson, Samuel CRITICISM, 5, 6;
DEATH, 5; DRINKING, 8, 9; EQUALITY, 2;
FREEDOM, 2; FRIENDSHIP, 5; GAMES, 5;
HUNTING, 2; IRELAND, 2, 3; KNOWLEDGE,
3, 4; LONDON, 1, 2; MARRIAGE, 2; MONEY,
5; OCCUPATIONS, 24, 25, 102; PATRIOTISM,
2; PLACES, 11, 12, 13; TRUST, 1;
WEDDINGS, 13; YOUTH, 4
Jonson, Ben SPEECH, 10
Jowett, Benjamin FAITH, 2; WORK, 5
Jung, Carl Gustav OCCUPATIONS,
116
Juvenal PUBLIC, 6

K

Kafka, Franz FREEDOM, 3
Keats, John BEAUTY, 1, 2; HUMAN
NATURE, 1; OCCUPATIONS, 74
Keller, Helen ENDURANCE, 1
Kemble, Charles TAXATION, 1
Kennedy, John Fitzgerald PEACE,
2; SPEECHES, 4
Kerr, Jean DRINKING, 10; MEDICINE, 2;
MONEY, 6
Key, Ellen WEDDINGS, 14
Khrushchev, Nikita BUSINESS, 6
Kierkegaard, Soren DEATH, 6
King, Martin Luther IDEALISM, 1
Kipling, Rudyard OBITUARIES, 2;
OCCUPATIONS, 103; SELF-CONTROL, 2;
SPEECH, 11; SPORT, 5
Kissinger, Henry ENEMIES, 1;
SPEECHES, 5
Knox, Ronald CHILDREN, 7, 8
Koestler, Arthur COURAGE, 2
Kolb, Barbara MUSIC, 6
Kristofferson, Kris FREEDOM, 4
Krutch, Joseph Wood HUNTING, 3

Shaw, George Bernard AGE, 20, 21, 22; ARGUMENTS, 4; ART, 6; DRINKING, 15; ECONOMICS, 2; EDUCATION, 10; ENVY, 1; EQUALITY, 3; EXCUSES, 3; HUNTING, 4; MONEY, 11; MORALITY, 6; OCCUPATIONS, 8, 105; PARTIES, 3; PLACES, 17, 18; SORROW, 2; SPEECHES, 25; TEMPTATION, 1; WEDDINGS, 20
Shawcross, Lord MORALITY, 7
Sheen, J. Fulton BUSINESS, 8
Sheppard, H. R. L. CHARITY, 2
Sheridan, Richard Brinsley APOLOGIES, 2; COMPLIMENTS, 6
Sherriff, R. C. LEAVING, 13
Shorter, Clement King OPTIMISM, 2
Singer, Isaac Bashevis FREEDOM, 6
Skelton, Red FUNERALS, 5
Slezak, Leo MISTAKES, 5
Smith, Adam BUSINESS, 9
Smith, Cyril GOVERNMENT, 2
Smith, Logan Pearsall MONEY, 12
Smith, Sydney BUSINESS, 10; HUNTING, 5; IGNORANCE, 2; MARRIAGE, 8; OCCUPATIONS, 29; PRAYER, 3; SPEECH, 15
Smollett, Tobias OCCUPATIONS, 106
Smythe, Tony CENSORSHIP, 2
Socrates GOOD, 5
Solzhenitsyn, Alexander ANIMALS, 4; POWER, 5
Southey, Robert YOUTH, 7
Spaak, Paul Henri AGREEMENT, 2
Spark, Muriel CHILDREN, 13; OCCUPATIONS, 94
Spenser, Edmund DEATH, 8
Stead, Christina SELF-MADE MEN, 3
Steffens, Lincoln FUTURE, 4
Sterne, Laurence OCCUPATIONS, 47
Stevas, Norman St John SNOBBERY, 2
Stevens, Alfred OCCUPATIONS, 19
Stevenson, Adlai COMPLIMENTS, 7; FAILURE, 2; OCCUPATIONS, 53, 87; SUCCESS, 5
Stevenson, Robert Louis ABSTINENCE, 6; FRIENDSHIP, 8
Steinbeck, John ADVICE, 3
Stockwood, Mervyn OCCUPATIONS, 95
Stone, I. F. AGE, 23
Stoppard, Tom ART, 7; DEMOCRACY, 3; OCCUPATIONS, 63
Stowe, Harriet Beecher ACHIEVEMENT, 6
Strindberg, August DOGS, 3
Surtees, R. S. HUNTING, 6

Swift, Jonathan AMBITION, 4; COURAGE, 4
Szasz, Thomas HAPPINESS, 3; OCCUPATIONS, 121

T

Taft, William Howard FAILURE, 3
Talleyrand FRIENDSHIP, 9
Temple, William SPORT, 10
Teresa, Mother CHARITY, 3
Thackeray, William Makepeace FAITH, 3; WEDDINGS, 21
Thatcher, Denis MEN AND WOMEN, 7
Thatcher, Margaret OCCUPATIONS, 88
Thiers, Louis Adolphe SNOBBERY, 3
Thomas, Edward PAST, 5
Thomas, Gwyn PLACES, 19
Thompson, William Hepworth IMPERFECTION, 3
Thomson, Joseph LONDON, 3
Thoreau, Henry David ADVICE, 4; ARGUMENTS, 5; TRUTH, 7
Thurber, James CRITICISM, 9; DECEPTION, 3; MARRIAGE, 9
Toscanini, Arturo MUSIC, 8
Tracy, Spencer POVERTY, 5
Trollope, Anthony PROPHECY, 1
Truffaut, François OCCUPATIONS, 9
Truman, Harry S. ECONOMICS, 3; RESPONSIBILITY, 2
Tucker, Sophie AGE, 24
Turenne, Vicomte de POWER, 6
Turnbull, Margaret FAMILY, 8; MEN AND WOMEN, 8
Twain, Mark EDUCATION, 11; ENEMIES, 2; FREEDOM, 7; INDECISION, 1; MANNERS, 2; MONEY, 13; OBITUARIES, 3; OCCUPATIONS, 26, 48; SPEECHES, 21; SPORT, 11; WOMEN, 11
Tynan, Kenneth COMPLIMENTS, 8; OCCUPATIONS, 38

U

Ustinov, Peter DIPLOMACY, 3; JEWS, 2; OCCUPATIONS, 107; OPTIMISM, 3

V

Vail, Amanda MEN, 4
Valéry, Paul OCCUPATIONS, 89
Vanbrugh, John WOMEN, 12